Contents

ACKNOWLEDGEMENTS

This book is dedicated to not one but many who in various capacities helped me in understanding love and human behaviour. Also, I include the many I love and have loved.

First and foremost, my better half deserves special thanks for loving me with all her heart, mind and soul. With her I share a companionate love.

My parents who always told me not to fall in love every time deserve thanks for their good counsel. Sorry mom and dad, I never did listen to you. I am still in love, in love with you all and...

And above all, I dedicate this piece of work to the most beautiful gift of love from God – my darling daughter, who has made me realise that the greatest of all loves is that between parents and their children. Always honour your mother and father, and the kingdom of love will be yours.

Dr. Amit Abraham

Rules of Attraction

GET THE LOVE OF ONE YOU ADMIRE

Dr. Amit Abraham

UNICORN BOOKS

Publisher
UNICORN BOOKS
F-2/16, Ansari Road, Daryaganj, New Delhi-110002
☎ 011-23275434, 23262683, 23250704 • *Fax:* 011-23257790
E-mail: info@unicornbooks.in • *Website:* www.unicornbooks.in

Branch : Mumbai
23-25, Zaoba Wadi, Thakurdwar, Mumbai-401002
☎ 022-22010941, 022-22053387
E-mail: rapidex@bom5.vsnl.net.in

Showroom :
★ **PM Publications,** New Delhi
- 10-B, Netaji Subhash Marg, Daryaganj
  New Delhi-110002
- 6686, Khari Baoli, Delhi-110006

ISBN 978-81-7806-151-1
Rules of Attraction

Edition: June 2013

Printed at : *Unique Color Carton, Mayapuri, New Delhi-110064*

PREFACE

Dear Readers,

There are many books available in the market and a lot of information available on the Internet about love, loving and getting the one you want. Getting the one you love is not a tactic; it is an understanding between two people looking forward to share their future life.

This book is unique because it focuses on the aspect of love from the standpoint of psychology. It gives you an insight into human behaviour, which is very essential when you are handling other people emotionally. It also tells you about the psychology of love because you need to evaluate yourself on this continuum from time to time. It finally tells you how to get the one you want.

I wish you all the best in your love life and hope this book will be useful to you. I sincerely request you not to misuse the guidance given in it. Love is pure and let it be so.

You can e-mail me your queries and comments at samvaidhna@hotmail.com, and as a professional psychologist I will be glad to counsel you.

Dr. Amit Abraham

OVERVIEW

Many people believe that they already know the essential facts and principles of behaviour – facts and principles that they have learned as a result of practical experience in dealing with people. They feel that they do not need any 'theoretical' or 'so-called scientific' knowledge. Unquestionably, these people have accumulated a great deal of practical information about how other people behave and, in a pragmatic sense, their knowledge of human nature may be adequate to handle many of their daily problems of business, administration, and normal social interaction. But it is just as obviously true that these men of affairs do not have the knowledge needed to evaluate behaviour, to understand fully and to love persons in totality – in the framework of psychological concepts.

There is an important difference between practical and scientific knowledge about behaviour. The major objective of science is not primarily to control and predict, but to understand. Effective control is a reward of understanding, and accuracy in prediction is a check on understanding. The African savage who tips his spear with poison and succeeds in killing his game or his enemy demonstrates some practical knowledge about the pharmacology of some toxic substances. However, no one would think of calling the savage a pharmacologist. He can control with some degree of accuracy, but he does not understand what he is doing or why his prediction is correct when it happens to be so. Like the African savage, many may assert that they do understand, but their 'understanding' fails to meet the requirements of science. The failure to differentiate between the scientific understanding of behaviour and practical know-how about behaviour has unfortunate consequences.

In order to understand and love one fully, it is essential to understand the basics of behaviour and not just get carried away by the overt acts of the one you intend to spend a lifetime with. To understand this, one must first know what behaviour is from a scientific point of view.

Behaviour can be defined in many ways. It can be defined as an observable activity of a specific organism, the measurable activity of a specific organism, the responses of an individual species or group to stimuli, a specific response of a specific organism, a part response of a response pattern, movement, or finally, the total activity – subjective and objective, non-observable and observable – of individual or group. In short, behaviour includes anything a person (or an animal) does that can be observed, recorded, and studied. No one ever saw or heard a mind, but we can see and hear behaviour. We can see and measure what a person does and hear and record what a person says (this is vocal behaviour). From what is done and said, we can and do make inferences about the feelings, attitudes, thoughts, and other mental processes, which may be behind the behaviour. In this way, internal mental events can be understood and given meaning through the external manifestations of people – their behaviour. Thus, it is through behaviour that we can actually come to understand internal mental processes that would otherwise be hidden from us.

To understand and evaluate behaviour in its totality, we have to break the entire process into its various components and establish a crystal-clear relationship amongst them, then only we will be able to understand and talk about the art of loving.

Behaviour is the Outcome of Stimulation

Behaviour is the outcome of a series of psychological and environmental reactions. It is the response to the multiple stimuli impinging upon the sensory organs of a person from time to time. The responses are selective and are based on past experiences as well as present evaluations of a specific situation. The stimulus, organism, environment, constitutional make-up, culture, emotions, attention, perception, etc., play a dominant and interrelated role in the final outcome of behaviour. As one cannot judge a book by its cover, similarly one can't just form a definite opinion by one's overt behaviour.

Empathy – A Must for Understanding

Another important and essential part in behaviour assessment and evaluation is the role played by empathy. Empathy means the understanding and sharing of another person's emotional experience in a particular situation. It can also be described as a process of 'feeling into' the emotions expressed in the movements or dynamic postures of people. The way to experience is primarily through linguistic communication, but it can also come through a spontaneous expression of feeling. In other words, empathy is the ability to put one's self in another's place to understand the other person's views and feelings (behaviour). Where there is no empathy, there is no love.

Empathy requires a receptive set (taking the role of the other), an appreciation of the meaning of the emotion-eliciting situation for the person, and an accurate interpretation of the person's verbal and non-verbal behaviour. The empathetic reaction can range from involuntary non-verbal and/or physiological responses to the experience of an emotion similar to that experienced by the other person. Non-verbal reactions have been associated with motor mimicry, the spontaneous and unconscious imitation of the facial movements and bodily postures. Physiological responses may include, for example, muscle tension and change in pulse rate or breathing.

All Our Knowledge has its Origins in Our Perceptions

Along with empathy, another important aspect is the one related with person perception. *Person perception refers to those processes by which we come to know and think about others – their characteristics, qualities, and inner states.* We view people as unitary entities (things) that possess various physical and personality features, thoughts and feelings. Our perception of people differs from our perception of inanimate objects in that we usually make inferences about the inner states of people. When we enter the presence of others, we typically try to 'size them up'. We look for cues – signs and signals – that give us crucial information about them. Psychologists have identified a number of key factors that influence this process by which we come to know and understand behaviour.

True Love is a Commitment

Now coming to love, the first thing I have to say is that true and lasting love is the outcome of a lifelong understanding between two individuals. True love develops gradually and is in sharp contrast with love at first sight. True love has three components: *intimacy, passion* and *commitment*. Intimacy refers to the closeness or bonding of two partners. Passion refers to the sexual drive and sexual arousal associated with love, and finally commitment refers to the decision that one is in love and the promise to maintain a loving relationship. If passion is the primary component, the relationship tends to be short-lived; intimacy and commitment are essential to a lasting relationship.

Why People fall in Love

Have you ever wondered as to why people fall in love? There seem to be two answers for the above question. First, some people fall in love to engage in sexual interaction with partners even in the absence of closeness, commitment, or emotional bonding. This is *passionate love* – an intense and often unrealistic emotional response to another person. The second category is of those for whom love not only includes a sexual relationship but also a feeling of closeness, commitment and emotional bonding. This type of love is akin to *companionate love* and is more lasting.

The Basis of Attraction

Another aspect related with love is the basis on which people get attracted to each other. We have a strong tendency to get attracted towards persons who are attractive, and forget that beauty is only skin deep. Remember that handsome is the one who does handsome.

Apparently, in real-life situations, we fear rejection and select partners who are most likely to reciprocate our advances. We generally experience the greatest payoff and the least cost when we direct our efforts towards someone of approximately equal physical attractiveness. A good deal of research reveals that we tend to like others who are similar to us. But at the same time, research also has indicated that complementary needs play a role in producing attraction. Complementary needs refer to two different personality traits that are the counterparts of each other and that provide a sense of completeness when they are joined. In either case, understanding is of prime importance. We have to search within the other what we are seeking, and if we find it then love begins to grow and finally mature into a long-term relationship.

Want to hear the Magic Words – Have Patience

Falling in love and getting the one you want is an art. To get the one you love to say 'yes' requires a lot of hard work. Remember that your actions peak louder than your words. The road is long and also lonesome at times, but remember, you have a dream to fulfil. Don't ever give up even if the pace is slow. You will surely succeed if your love is true.

The first step to get the one you want is to understand that person inside out. The person should be like an open book for you. After having understood the person, the process of intrusion begins. We start from the public zone and move strategically till we are successful in intruding into the intimate zone of the person we so desire. Finally, and hopefully, you will get the one you love to say 'yes' to you a thousand times.

I wish you all the best but request you not to misuse the knowledge you gain through this book to satisfy your evil needs. Let love be pure and let it inspire mankind. Let it remain the greatest weapon that all mankind trusts. □□

THE STARTERS

'The first impression is the last impression' is no doubt an old saying but I don't fully agree with it. It is like judging a book by its cover rather than its contents. Also, all that glitters is not necessarily gold. It can be diamond – artificial or real. Beauty is in the eyes of the beholder, but with the passage of time, the valleys beyond start looking greener. Love at first sight may last only a few nights. To meet, to know, to love and to part is a sad tale of many a human heart just because they never really loved. Why does one have to pass through conflicting stages in relationships, be they official, personal or casual? The answer is that one never understood the basic components that make a relationship work.

Be Slow and Steady if You Want to Win

Generally people jump into relationships without weighing the pros and cons. They lack basic understanding about each other, yet enter into a relationship. This should not be the technique. I personally am in favour of being slow and steady in forming opinions about others. *A good start is half the battle won.* But alas! Most of the people lose at the end though they think they had started out well. Life sure is queer with its many twists and turns; and many a failure in love turn about and victory is there for those who have the knowledge and understanding of human behaviour.

Stimulation and the Romantic Idol – Are You the One?

Now our *first step towards understanding behaviour will begin with the basic source of stimulation*. Newton's law says that a body will remain at rest or in uniform motion unless and until acted upon by an external force. The same law of inertia applies to a large extent with respect to human behaviour. This, in our context, refers to a stimulus. A stimulus is a variation in physical energy, inside or outside an organism, capable of influencing the afferent nervous system through receptors. Thus, a sensation corresponds to every external stimulus. The entire process, from the activation of a receptor up to sensation, is known as stimulus processing. However, an important aspect pertains to the intensity of the stimulus. For a stimulus to be effective and response to be produced, the stimulus must be well within the sensory limits of an individual.

In short, a stimulus evokes a sensation. A sensation is produced by external or internal stimuli acting on the sensory organs. A stimulus impinges – usually after passing through an organ that carries stimuli – on a specific sensory receptor cell, which becomes excited if the energy of the stimulus is above the threshold. That is why when you see someone attractive, your senses are stirred up and you find them stimulating.

In order to know the world around as well as within, physical energy (stimulus) must be changed into activity within the nervous system. The process of converting physical energy into nervous system activity is called transduction. Transduction occurs at the receptors – cells that are specialised for the most efficient conversion of one kind of energy to another. In general, during the transduction process, receptor cells convert physical energy into an electric voltage, or potential, called the receptor potential. In some sensory systems, the receptor potential itself directly triggers the nerve impulses that travel to the brain or spinal cord. In other sensory systems, the receptor potential leads to further electrical events, which in turn triggers nerve impulses. In either case, the electrical event that triggers nerve impulses is known as the generator potential.

For a given event (read person) in the environment, thousands of nerve impulses are generated and conducted to the central nervous system. Since these impulses travel along many different nerve fibres at slightly different times, they form a pattern of input to the central nervous system that is the basis of our sensory experience. Thus, beginning with the transduction process at the receptor, physical energy results in a pattern of nerve impulses in the central nervous system. In other words, the physical energy is changed into a code made up of a pattern of nerve firings. The firing patterns that correspond to events in the environment are known as afferent codes.

So now you know what exactly happens when you see someone. But whether the stimulation you receive will positively affect you depends on your own mental make-up.

Every individual has a romantic ideal, an image of the one that one is searching and longing for. If the image matches with the stimulation being received, then there are chances of further currents being generated. But mind it, for a magnetic effect to be produced, the stimulation must be the same at the other end also.

Be the Focus of Attention

There are many fish in the ocean of love but why do we perceive only a few as worthy. The answer lies in the process of attention.

At a given moment, our sense organs are bombarded by a multitude of stimuli, yet we perceive only a few of them clearly. *Attention is the term given to the perceptual processes that select certain inputs for inclusion in our conscious experience, or awareness, at any given time*. The process of attention divides our field of experience into a focus and a margin. Events (persons) that we perceive clearly are at the focus of experience. Other items are perceived dimly; we may be aware of their presence, but only vaguely. These items are in the margin of attention. However, at some point one becomes aware of the marginal inputs and highlights another characteristic of attention, which it is constantly shifting. What is at the focus one moment may be in the margin the next and what is in the margin may become the focus. *So mind it, if you are trying to woo someone, always try to remain in the focus of their attention* or else a margin may be drawn even before you start entering into their social or personal zone.

How to be the Focus of Attention

Points to Remember

Now how does one go about being in the focus of another's attention? *Attention is generally captured and maintained by the features of the environment as well as by the motives and other physical and psychological conditions of the observer.* The stimuli that comprise the environment at any given instant are constant and insistent. These stimuli rarely reach the sense organs one by one. Most of these stimuli compete with other stimuli for attention (watch out, you have competition) or come linked with other stimuli that a person perceives as patterns (the person concerned must be wanting to have the best of all worlds and thus looking for a combination of all the best things). However, don't get disheartened because certain factors determine attention and you are one of the lucky few to know about them. These factors are the characteristics of the stimulus (your characteristics in this case), the internal needs (the needs of the other person), expectancies and past experiences (of the other person). These factors normally influence one's attention to an object or an event.

Several ***external factors*** also contribute to what one may attend to at any given moment. Among the important external factors that affect attention are nature of stimuli, location of stimuli, size of stimuli, intensity of stimuli, colour of stimuli, motion, contrast and novelty.

1. ***Nature of stimuli*** means whether the stimulus is visual or auditory, and whether it involves words or pictures, people or animals. Research has shown that a visual stimuli has chances of catching one's attention more than an auditory one. So the next time you pick up the phone with the intention of impressing someone put it back, dress up and make yourself visible before that person and then speak your heart out.
2. ***Location*** also plays an important role in the process of attention. If you are trying to move from the public zone into the social zone of the individual, then locate yourself as such that the person you are

trying to impress can receive the stimulations being sent by you.

3. Also see your ***background***. Let not there be many attractive people around you or else attention may keep fluctuating.

4. The ***intensity*** with which you are trying to impress also matters a lot. Intense stimuli have greater attention- catching power than weaker ones. Shy persons may be losers because they cannot openly express themselves with the required intensity. But if you are shy, don't get dejected. Maybe you are killing others softly with your charms. Also remember that brighter colours are more likely to attract attention than dull ones. So try to dress up accordingly.

5. ***Motion*** is another important determinant of attention. Human beings are quite sensitive to moving objects. Moving objects are easy to get attended to than stationary ones. Any change in the existing forces in the environment tends to attract

attention. So don't just sit and chat. Verbal expressions are important but gestures and signals will keep the attention of the other person centred on you.

6. *Novelty* of the stimulus is also of prime importance. Any unusual or irregular event is liable to gain more attention than a routine, usual event. So try to be novel in presentation, your talks and actions.

Besides the external factors in the environment that influence attention, there are factors within the individual that are important determinants of attention. These are motivation, interests, attitudes and prejudices, fatigue and preparatory set.

1. *Motivation* is one important factor in determining which stimulus elicits attention. Physical or social deprivations related to basic human needs have a strong effect on the direction and intensity of attention. The fact that in identical circumstances people show great differences in the degree to which

they attend to a particular stimulus is partly due to their motivational state at a given instance. So make sure to try and identify the needs of the person whose attention you are trying to attract so that he/she may be motivated to attend to you.

2. One's *interests* also influence attention. Events or objects in which a person has already developed an interest are more likely to attract attention than objects and events in which there has been no interest initially. Now firstly you have to find out the interest areas of the person you are seeking and then indulge in them. This way you will surely attract their attention.

3. *Attitudes* and ***prejudices*** also affect the extent to which an individual is inclined to pay attention to events or ideas. Hence make sure that you fall in line with the attitudinal thinking of the ones whose love you are seeking.

4. Physical and mental ***fatigue*** has a detrimental effect on attentiveness. As a person becomes physically

fatigued, there occurs a reduction in his vigilance in any sense modality. So you should identify the right time to be on target or else you will goof.

5. One of the major factors that make a person attend to one stimulus instead of another is his *preparatory set*. Preparatory set refers to the predisposition to act in certain ways and the readiness of an individual to respond to one kind of stimuli and not to the other kinds. Individuals also vary in their responses to the same stimuli because of their habitual or momentary interests that prepare them for certain kinds of stimuli. Preparatory set or expectancy determines what a person attends to. His attention is directed towards those objects or events that he is set to receive. So if you are trying to catch someone's attention, make sure to know what is running in that person's mind at that moment. Whether he or she is mentally prepared to be receptive of the advances you are making or not. Don't try to force yourself into that

individual's presence or you may rub him/her the wrong way.

Your Kind Attention Please

In short, we can say that attention is a pre-perceptive process that depends upon one's interest and motivation as well as the nature of stimuli impinging upon him. *Thus, the first and most important aspect is to catch the attention of the person you wish to court.* If proper attention is not paid, the signals that you are trying to send will not be accurately logged in the short-term memory store of the concerned individual, and when he/she tries to put the threads together, he/she may be missing out on vital information needed to form an impression about you. This is so because only that information is stored in the short-term memory store which is attended to. This information is transferred to the long-term store on repeated elaborate rehearsal. This elaborate rehearsal is not just a mechanical process but also involves giving meaning and organisation to information. So make sure to repeat your performance of attention-catching till you are able to enter into a long-term association with that person. But mind it, your attention-seeking behaviour should not be meaningless.

The aspect of attention is not only important in the starting stages but is also a permanent requirement if a relationship is to be enjoyed in its totality.

Understand how Meaning is read from Sensory Signals

After attention comes the part of perception. Perception refers to the apparently direct and immediate knowledge of the world, and also of our own bodies, by neural signals from the sense organs. We usually think of our own perceptions as our consciousness of the world around us, and of ourselves, but much of the perception by which behaviour is initiated and controlled is totally unconscious, and awareness of the perception of things and states of affairs by which we act is never more than fragmentary.

Perception is essentially the reading of meaning from sensory signals, so that behaviour is, generally, appropriate to all manner of hidden characteristics of objects and situations, and is not merely triggered and guided by the stimulus that happens to be available.

Thus perception may be defined as the process by which the sensory input or information is organised and interpreted into a meaningful experience.

Senses are crucial to perception. Humans have at least ten sensory channels: vision, hearing, taste, smell, touch, cold, warmth, pain, kinesthesis (muscle, tendon and joint sense) and the sense of balance (equilibratory sense). Objects and events in the environment activate the sense receptors by physical energies and this activation creates a movement of the nerve impulse to the brain where this impulse is processed and interpreted. Objects and events are perceived after all these processes.

As with the case of attention, perception also has its determinants. These are attention, preparatory set, motivation, cognitive style and value.

What Determines Your Perception

1. ***Attention*** here refers to the perceptual focussing. In fact, we do not react equally to all the stimuli at a time but rather focus upon a few, selecting certain messages from the constant jumble of sensory information. Individual differences are also present when it comes to paying attention.

2. We often prepare ourselves to perceive and act upon stimuli that we expect to appear. Such a preparation is termed as ***preparatory set***, which particularly is an anticipatory adjustment holding certain kinds of responses in readiness.

3. Perceptual progress depends largely on the individual's particular ***motivation***. It is likely that the individuals who are in a state of need may perceive the objects in the same manner that may satisfy their need. That is why, as also mentioned before, it is essential to identify the need of the individual. Further, the person you are trying to impress may be in need of emotional and loving

warmth and will perceive your advances as fruitful. If that is the case then you are in luck.

4. Individuals have their own ***cognitive style*** in dealing with the environment. Generally people use two approaches in perceiving the environment. The first is *field-dependent* and the other *field-independent*. In the first approach, the environment is perceived as a whole. In the second approach, the elements of the environment are perceived as separate and distinct from each other and tend to draw each element as standing out from a background. Thus, people differ in the ways they typically and characteristically process information. Among the many dimensions along which people vary in perceptual-cognitive style are firstly, the degree to which their perceptions and other aspects of their behaviour and personality are flexible or constricted and secondly, their field-dependence or field-independence. People whose perceptions are at the flexible end of the flexible-constricted

dimension are said to have a wider focus of attention, to be less affected by interfering influences, and to be less dominated by internal needs and motives than are people at the constricted end.

5. *Values* also play an important role in the perceptual process of an individual. Values are acquired through experience. They are the link between needs and action, and they serve to allocate attention and efforts to various needs. Thus, a person is more likely to perceive objects, events or situations, which he considers good or beneficial to his well-being.

Thus perception is more than a matter of reflexes, for it uses subtle 'cues'of many kinds to make inferences to what the objects around us are like, and it is predictive. To be predictive in unusual situations, it has to draw intelligent analogies from a rich store of generalised knowledge of the world. This cognitive, knowledge-based aspect of perception allows appropriate intelligent behaviour even when there is little information available from the senses, and even our eyes, which probably command more of the brain than all the other senses, cannot transmit anything like so much information in 'real time'as they seem to do.

No wonder it's said that love is blind. But beware, most of us do have a sixth sense that warns and tells us, apart from other things, about the intentions of other persons. So don't try to put on a mask before the one you are seeking as that individual may be seeing right through it and will form a negative opinion about you. I personally believe in the age-old saying that honesty is the best policy and love should always be honest.

The Importance of Observation – Reading the Signals

Apart from the sensory processes, an important aspect related to the process of understanding and evaluating objects, situations, events, behaviour, etc., is the process of observation. Observation is a methodically controlled, non-random, purposive examination of the action of one or several individuals in order to discover something characteristic about their personality.

Observation is a very essential and crucial step in understanding human behaviour. It helps us to know what people do and how they differ in their behaviour. Further, the causes of the observed behaviour can be found.

When we are trying to impress someone, it is essential that we observe that person and try to read the signals being sent by him/her and then act in accordance. Thus, we must always keep our eyes wide open and look for cues which are important for future developments.

This brings us to the close of this chapter. Attention, perception as well as observation are important steps and stages in the preliminary rounds of your efforts towards the attainment of your goal: **getting the one you want.** □□

FIRST IMPRESSIONS

How do we come to know other people? Our first impressions of others are initially based on the information we obtain about them and, in some instances, the inferences we make about the cause for their behaviour. When we have only a limited amount of information available, we tend to fill in the gaps to arrive at a fairly complete and comprehensive image of the individual in question.

Forming impressions of other people is probably so natural and a habitual game everyone is involved in, consciously or unconsciously. Impression formation is a process by which information about others is converted into more or less enduring cognitions or thoughts about them. When we first meet someone, we have access to considerable information – how the person looks, and what he or she does and says. According to one point of view, we are not overwhelmed by the abundance of this information because we are able to group it into categories that predict things of importance to us. These categories and their perceived interrelationships form the basic cognitive framework by which we understand others. The linkages among these categories will determine what predictions we make about someone when we have only limited information. If, for example, you think people who wear glasses are intelligent, then whenever you meet a stranger wearing glasses, you will be disposed to believe that he or she is highly intelligent. All categories are related to some other categories and unrelated to many more. In your mind, wearing glasses might also be related to 'timidity' but not to 'honesty' or 'sense of humour'. By generating predictions, or expectations, we can efficiently interact with other people even when we possess only minimal information about them.

Of course there is no guarantee that a given piece of information will be categorised in the same way by different people. You have probably had the experience of finding that your first impressions of a person differ markedly from those of your friends. There is evidence that people vary in the way they tend to evaluate others on meeting them the first time. One such difference is that some people are predisposed to like everyone they meet. They may focus on the desirable characteristics of others and search for evidence that people possess certain favourable traits. Others have a tendency to dislike people on their first meeting and may try to discover the existence of undesirable characteristics.

The categories we use and their assumed interrelationships constitute our template or framework for understanding the world in which we live. This framework, in essence, is our theory about how things are supposed to work.

Understanding Others – Their Traits

For understanding other people, the category most frequently used is the *trait*. Traits are classification schemes for describing the behaviour of individuals. Our language provides us with many options for describing behaviour, such as assertive, friendly, punctual, or talkative. Traits are a compelling set of categories used to describe, remember, and communicate our own and other person's behaviour. Traits are also perceived to be interrelated; they seem to occur in clusters. You might, for example, assume that people who are assertive are also ambitious or that intelligent people are also industrious. This assumed relationship among traits is called implicit personality theory, a name that underscores how our own cognitive framework generates predictions about other people that go beyond the information available to us. Implicit personality theories help us to simplify the information we receive in social interaction, colour the way we interpret events, and guide our responses to other people.

Once you meet someone, you settle on a group of traits you observe and assume that person to have the same. To make this decision, you must make a judgement about how favourable you feel towards the person. One procedure you might follow is to add the favourable traits together. If you do this, you will have a more positive impression if you think a person is both kind and honest than if you think the person is simply kind. On the other hand, you might average these two pieces of information, in which case your impression would remain about the same – the average of the two favourable traits would be close to the value of each of them alone. The averaging model is probably closer to what you would actually do, except that it would not be so simple. Instead, certain pieces of information would be seen as more important and thus would be weighted more heavily than others; your overall impression would represent a weighted average of the information you have about that person. One thing you would consider is the relevance of the information for the particular judgement you are making. You assign importance to different characteristics in assessing different persons. Information obtained first also seems to be weighted more heavily. Most people believe there is some value in making a good first impression, and research shows that such efforts are not wasted; a primacy effect does often occur in impression formation. Furthermore, we generally give more importance to information concerning negative traits than to information concerning positive traits that others might possess. Each of these factors affects the importance people give to various pieces of information when forming an impression of another person.

How to Evaluate – An Evaluation Exercise

Now how does one go about doing this evaluation work? A list of adjectives is given in *Table 1* with the help of which we can measure the tendency to evaluate others in a positive or negative fashion. Before reading further, check the 12 characteristics that concern you in

TABLE I

Sincere (H)	Solemn (M)
Honest (H)	Proud (M)
Understanding (H)	Prudent (M)
Trustworthy (H)	Shrewd (M)
Intelligent (H)	Materialistic (M)
Open-minded (H)	Eccentric (M)
Friendly (H)	Boring (L)
Gentle (H)	Touchy (L)
Courteous (H)	Boastful (L)
Tactful (H)	Conceited (L)
Well-read (H)	Phony (L)
Witty (H)	Childish (L)
Authoritative (M)	Nosey (L)
Self-possessed (M)	Snobbish (L)
Sceptical (M)	Hostile (L)
Forceful (M)	Finicky (L)
Conservative (M)	Stingy (L)
Nonchalant (M)	Complaining (L)

evaluating others. (For the moment, ignore the letters that follow the traits).

Now go back and count the number of H's, M's, and L's on the traits you checked. They stand for high, medium, or low in likeability. If you have a majority of H's, you probably tend to view people favourably on meeting them the first time.

If most of the adjectives you checked are L's, you are likely to have unfavourable first impressions of others.

It has been found that certain personality variables may influence our initial evaluations of others. Individuals use different dimensions when they evaluate others. Their evaluations are based on their own motives, emotions, interests, and personality make-up.

Impression Formation and Physical Attractiveness

Another aspect that plays an important role in impression formation is physical attractiveness. Physical attractiveness is the combination of facial features, physique and grooming that is perceived as aesthetically appealing by members of a given culture at a given time period.

When we first meet someone, we are likely to notice his or her physical appearance before anything else. While you have been warned before not to judge a book by its cover, considerable research has demonstrated that one does just that. We have a strong tendency to be favourably impressed by attractive people and to be less favourably impressed with those who are not so attractive. One thing we must keep in mind while discussing about physical attractiveness is that beauty lies in the beholder's eye and the criterion of physical attractiveness is gender specific

Generally What Type of Women Attract Men

Though there is no universal standard of beauty with respect to the human body, research has shown that men are attracted to either woman, one who has childlike features, large wide-spaced eyes, a small nose and chin, or the one who has prominent cheek bones, narrow cheeks, high eyebrows, large pupils and a big smile. These are two facial types to which men are more attracted regardless of the women being white, black or oriental. Other aspects of attractiveness in women include medium-sized breasts, a slim figure, shapely legs and delicate feet and toes.

Generally What Type of Men Attract Women

On the other hand, females are physically attracted to men with prominent cheek bones, large chin, wide shoulders and large chest. Recent research has shown that the face of Mr. Right may change from week to week. It was found that a woman's preferences for male features changes at different stages of the menstrual cycle. When women are more likely to conceive, they are more receptive to men with more rugged 'masculine features'. During the other three weeks of the month, when the odds of getting pregnant are lower, including during the menstrual period, women choose faces that are smoother and more 'effeminate'.

How Partners are Chosen – The Matching Hypothesis

In hypothetical situations, research shows that we think in terms of idealised visions and prefer individuals who possess considerable physical attractiveness. Very simple, physical beauty seems to be rewarding for both sexes, both as an individual experience and for the reflected status it brings. But the supply of unusually beautiful or handsome partners is limited. Real-life situations generally confirm the matching hypothesis of mate selection, namely, that we tend to choose partners whose degree of physical attractiveness is similar to our own.

We would ideally like to associate with beautiful or handsome people, but in practice we reduce our aspirations.

Apparently, in real-life situations, we fear rejection and select partners who are most likely to reciprocate our advances. We generally experience the greatest payoff and the least cost when we direct our efforts towards someone of approximately equal physical attractiveness.

Similarity Leads To Liking – Why?

A good deal of research reveals that we tend to like others who are similar to us. Why should this be so; why should similarity lead to liking? There are many reasons. People strive for cognitive consistency among their attitudes and behaviour. People who agree on important matters will become attracted to each other because they satisfy one another's needs for consistency. We may also be attracted to others who are similar to us because we assume they will like us. And being liked can in turn produce liking for the would-be friend. When we perceive others as similar to us, it encourages us to expect more positive outcomes from interaction with them. Also, when we find others who hold similar attitudes, we are attracted to them because they validate our own.

Interpersonal Attraction is also based on Complementary Needs

According to Newton's third law of motion, every action has an equal and opposite reaction. However, the universal law of magnetism states that unlike poles attract. Both these laws also hold true in the case of attractiveness. People with some personality traits 'rub us the wrong way', while we feel comfortable with those who have certain other traits. Research has indicated that complementary needs play a role in producing attraction. Stress here is laid on difference rather than similarities. Complementary needs refer to two different personality traits that are the counterparts of each other and that provide a sense of completeness when they are joined. They mutually supply each other's lack. Although the theory includes attraction between friends of the same or opposite sex, it is seen most clearly in the area of mate selection. We typically seek within the field of eligible mates a person who gives the greatest promise of providing us with the maximum gratification of our needs.

Many of our needs are met in a complementary manner. People who possess a strong desire for recognition may love and be loved by differential people who prefer to bask in the achievements of others. Within such relationships, each person finds his or her needs satisfied. People with a nurturance need – a need to sympathise with or help others in difficulty – find fulfilment with people having a succorance need – a need to be helped and taken care of. Dominant people find a complementary relationship with submissive people. Talkative people find themselves attracted to taciturn people. Sadists find a reciprocal sense of satisfaction and well-being with masochists. However, interpersonal attraction based on complementary needs depends upon the extent to which individuals both gratify one another's social needs and fulfil the obligations of the role context in which the relationship existed.

Universal Law of Interpersonal Attraction

Although the theory of complementary needs appears to find confirmation in everyday life, actual studies have produced mixed findings. While a number support the theory, others fail to confirm it. One problem is that some of our personality needs are complemented by similarity rather than by contrast. *Thus a combination of similarity and contrast, in varying degree, plays an important role in interpersonal attraction.*

The Role of Attribution in Attractiveness

Apart from outward beauty, attribution also plays an important role in determining our attractiveness. How we judge persons when we first meet them has a lot to do with our initial feelings towards them.

To characterise other people in terms of certain traits, intentions, or abilities require us to make attributions, or inferences, about them. Because we do not have access to the personal thoughts, motives, or feelings of others, we make inferences about these traits based on the behaviour we observe. By making such attributions from certain behaviours, we are able to increase our ability to predict how a person will behave in the future.

Attributions are important because the causes we attribute to the behaviour of others can influence our own behaviour as well. To illustrate, suppose you arrive at a party and see an attractive woman/handsome man sitting alone. In speculating about why that person is sitting alone, two possibilities may occur to you – the person concerned may not know anyone else at the party and, being somewhat reserved, may be reluctant to initiate conversation with others. Or, she/he may simply be waiting for her/his date to arrive. If you settle on the first attribution, you may very well walk over and introduce yourself to that person. If you decide the second attribution to be more likely, then you may begin to look around for someone else irrespective of the physical appeal of that person.

The Attribution Advantage

One advantage of attribution is that it takes into account the situational factors involved. Much of the earlier discussion on first impressions focussed on characteristics of the observed or the observer and ignored environmental factors. Attribution suggests that the situation a person is in can have an important effect on how the other person is perceived.

Internal and External Attributions

There are two types of attributions: personal or internal attributions, and environmental or external attributions. Let's take an example to explain these. Suppose a stranger in a restaurant trips over an end table and spills your tea. If you view him as clumsy, then this will be your personal attribution. But if you blame the furniture arrangement for this mishap, it will be an environmental attribution.

Several studies have found that people tend to make personal attributions for the undesirable behaviour of others, and to make environmental attributions for similar behaviour of their own. Conversely, people tend to make environmental attributions for the success of others, and personal attributions for their own success. Thus if we get into an argument with someone, we assume that they are aggressive and hostile, and that we are forced by the situation to defend our position.

Attributions and Personality Characteristics

The attributions one makes can vary depending on certain personality characteristics. Individuals with high levels of self-esteem tend to follow the pattern described above. If they are successful in a particular task, they make personal attributions, and if they fail, they make environmental attributions. Individuals low in self-esteem tend to do just the opposite. It appears that those with low self-esteem cannot believe anything good about themselves, while those with high self-esteem cannot believe anything bad about themselves.

The Result of Impression Formation

In a final analysis of this chapter, we can say that the process by which we form impressions of others are efficient means for guiding our reactions to others. Our impressions are grounded in our observations of others – their physical characteristics and their behaviour in particular settings. Our observations provide the information that is converted into meaningful inferences by our cognitive framework. At a minimum, this process involves placing the information into cognitive categories, which are related to other categories. We can, thus, make simple inferences from minimum data or combine rich sets of information into overall impressions. Under some circumstances, we can also make inferences about the cause of other people's behaviour as well as our own behaviour. Despite the smoothness by which the process works, however, it does not guarantee accuracy or comparability with other's observations. We each make a personal contribution to the process because we may have different ways of categorising the information, individual aspects to our cognitive framework, or some unique way of combining information. ***Nevertheless, the end result of impression formation determines how we react to others and how we see ourselves.*** □□

BEAUTY AND THE BEHOLDER

It's truly said that beauty lies in the eyes of the beholder. Our eyes are just one of the sense organs and any soothing stimulus brings about pleasing sensations. But mind it, sensations alone do not account for evaluating others, be it beauty or anything else. The eyes are God's gift not only to see but also feel.

For many of us, the most interesting objects of perception in our environment are other people. In our everyday interaction with other persons, we frequently assess their intentions and motives with respect to us. We determine whether or not a person likes us and our judgement of his feelings guides our own reaction towards him. In situations where another person is attempting to influence us, we try to fathom his intentions and his sincerity.

Opinions are Formed through Information

Often an opinion concerning the other person is not based on direct observation of him but on statements by others or on knowledge of who he is. Moreover, opinions, evaluations, or feelings involve subjective judgement and inference that go beyond the kind of direct sensory impressions that characterise perception. Thus, *we have to try and see within an individual to get to know him/her better.*

Forming Basic Impressions about Others

In everyday life, impressions and judgements of other persons are formed in widely varying situations. These situations vary in three major respects: Firstly, the amount of information available to the perceiver for the purpose of forming a judgement concerning the other person. Secondly, the extent of interaction between the perceiver and the other person; and finally, the degree to which the relation between the perceiver and the other person is a well-established one.

When we are introduced to a person, our information is often very limited, our interaction is restricted, and no established relation exists. We obtain only a brief glimpse of his appearance and hear him speak only a few conventional phrases, yet we may form a definite impression of his personality. When we perceive and judge a person, we have three things. First, information about the person such as, physical appearance, expressive and other motor behaviour, verbal behaviour, etc. Second is the information about ourselves, our values, attitudes, beliefs, feelings, in short, our own personality. This is important since we perceive and judge others on the basis of the type of person we are. The third is related with the environment, i.e. whether some situational factor is operating behind the behaviour being observed. Largely on the basis of these three things, we are able to form basic impressions about others.

The different modes of perceiving others may be described in terms of a dimension varying from the simple to the complex. Since perceptual experiences are private, no one can directly perceive the experience of another individual. A person is perceived simply in terms of outward appearance or superficial characteristics, e.g. his/her body build, facial features, and mannerisms, or mainly in terms of a central trait and its immediate ramifications, e.g. a withdrawn person may be perceived as shy, quiet, retiring, etc., or in terms of a cluster of congruous traits, i.e., traits which seem to belong together. For example, a large, strong man may be perceived as having a powerful voice and as being aggressive, self-confident, and forceful. And finally, in terms of a variety of traits including some which are incongruous, i.e. traits which seem not to belong together. A person may be perceived as kind, thoughtful, dishonest, and unsocial.

We often find other persons quite puzzling. They say and do things we don't expect, have motives we don't understand, and seem to see the world through eyes very different from our own. Yet we often at the same time engage in efforts to understand them – to gain insight into their intentions, traits, and motives. We try to figure out what other persons are really like, why they do and say the things they do. Then, on the basis of that knowledge, we try to determine the best ways of interacting with them.

The Process of Understanding – Moving into the Zones

The process of understanding others is a move from public to social to personal and finally to the intimate zone. This process of understanding is largely divided into two halves which run parallel to each other. First, we try to understand the other person's current feelings, moods, and emotions – how they are feeling here and now. Such information is often provided by *non-verbal cues* from the facial expressions, eye contact, body posture, and movements. Second, we attempt to understand the more lasting causes behind others' actions – their traits, motives, and intentions. Information relating to this is acquired through attribution. Attribution is a complex process in which we observe others' behaviour and then attempt to infer the causes behind it from various cues. (*Refer to the chapter on First Impressions.*)

Beware – Temporary Factors may influence Behaviour

In most cases, behaviour is strongly influenced by temporary factors or causes. Shifting moods, fleeting emotions, fatigue, illness, various drugs – all can influence the ways in which we think and behave. Many of us are more than willing to do favours for others when in a good mood. On the other hand, the reverse is true. Similarly, many people are more likely to lose their tempers and lash out at others in some manner when feeling irritable than when feeling mellow.

The Non-Verbal Cues for Understanding

Most of the time people tend to conceal their true feelings and it becomes difficult to assess the exact state of their mind. Yet, with certain observational methods, we can see through them. We can obtain revealing information about their inner feelings and reactions by paying careful attention to their non-verbal behaviour – changes in facial expression, eye contact, posture, body movements, and other expressive actions. Such behaviour is relatively irrepressible, that is, difficult to control, so even when others try to control their inner feelings, these often leak out in many ways through non-verbal cues. Non-verbal behaviours constitute a silent but eloquent language. The basic non-verbal communication channels that transmit key information about our inner emotional and affective states are facial expressions, eye contact, body movements and posture, and touching.

The Face – A Human Barometer

A person's face is usually a barometer of his emotions. It is possible to learn much about others' current moods and feelings from their facial expressions. In fact, six different basic emotions are represented clearly, and that too from a very early age, on the human face: anger, fear, sadness, disgust, happiness, and surprise. But this does not imply that human beings are capable of demonstrating only six different facial expressions. On the contrary, emotions occur in many combinations. Also, these reactions can vary greatly in strength.

When individuals experience various emotions, electrical activity in specific facial muscles increases, and when they move these muscles into the patterns of specific facial expressions, they show distinctive shifts in physiological reactions.

When under the influence of emotion, the facial expression of the person is the first to be altered. It is easiest to read the emotions of love and hate from the face. No amount of effort can successfully disguise the facial contortions in strong emotion from an experienced observer. In pleasant emotions, it is said that the face lights up with delight, this lighting up refers to the muscular expansion. Similarly, it is said that the face hangs down.

Here, the reference is to the contraction of the muscles. Prevalent sayings such as blushing with shame or averting the eyes, expansion of the eyes in fear, elevation of the eyebrows in anger, etc., are used to describe the changes in facial expressions in emotions.

The Eyes – Windows to the Soul

Other than the face, the eyes also provide important cues to emotions. The eyes are said to be the windows to the soul. We learn much about others feelings from their eyes. We interpret a high level of gazing from another as a sign of liking or friendliness. On the other hand, if others avoid eye contact with us, we may conclude that they are unfriendly, don't like us, or are simply shy.

While a high level of eye contact from others is usually interpreted as a sign of liking or positive feelings, there is one important exception to this general rule. If another person gazes at us continuously and maintains such contact regardless of any actions we perform, she or he can be said to be staring. A stare is often interpreted as a sign of anger or hostility, consider the phrase – a cold stare – and most people attempt to minimise their exposure to this particular kind of non-verbal communication when possible. Staring is one form of non-verbal behaviour that should be used with great caution in most situations.

In given light conditions, the pupils dilate or contract as a person's attitude and mood changes from positive to negative and vice-versa. When someone becomes excited, his pupils can dilate up to four times their normal size. Conversely, an angry, negative mood causes the pupils to contract to what are commonly known as 'beady little eyes' or 'snake eyes'. The area of the other person's body upon which the gaze is directed can have a powerful effect on the outcome of any face-to-face encounter.

The Voice – The Richest Cue

The adult human voice is even richer than the face and eyes in varieties of emotional expression. Change in inflection, loudness, pitch, or timbre may be used to express various types of emotional experiences. A rising inflection, for instance, generally conveys a feeling of surprise, doubt or incredulity. The rising, then falling inflection shows sarcasm. A slow, dragging monotone expresses defeat and dejection. A loud, hoarse, staccato speech with much variation in pitch suggests excitement.

Patterns of emotional expression, present in childhood, become increasingly clear-cut as the vocal apparatus matures. While these patterns appear to have an innate basis, they are complicated by learning and social imitation. That is, the precise 'tone of voice' associated with a particular emotional reaction is determined in part by social convention, although the higher pitch and strident tones associated with anger are undoubtedly inborn. The increase in body tension causes more tension in the vocal cords, thus 'raising' the voice. Quavering and stuttering are evidently native expressions of fear, and are frequently imitated by the actor who wants to convey a feeling of fear to the audience.

Actions Speak Louder than Words

Our current moods or emotions are often reflected in the position, posture, and movement of our bodies. Together, such non-verbal behaviours are termed as *body language*, and they too can provide us with several useful kinds of information about others.

Large number of movements, especially the ones in which one part of the body does something to another part, (e.g., touching, scratching, rubbing, etc.), suggest emotional arousal. The greater the frequency of such behaviour, the higher the level of arousal or nervousness seems to be. The specific movements made, too, can be revealing. We will discuss these in detail in the next chapter.

Touch Me – Touch Me Not

Touching is the most intimate non-verbal cue. It reflects a move from the personal to the intimate zone. Depending on various factors, a touch can suggest affection, sexual interest, dominance, caring, or even aggression. When one person touches another in a manner that is considered acceptable in the current context, positive reactions generally result. Thus, being touched in an innocuous, non-threatening way generates positive reactions. However, touching does not always produce such effects. If it is perceived as a status or power play, or if it is too prolonged, or too intimate in a context where such intimacy is not warranted, touching may evoke anxiety, anger, and other negative reactions.

Touching is strongly affected by social context and by cultural rules dictating who can touch whom and when. Another aspect is that of gender differences. In public places, males are more likely to touch females than vice-versa.

Appearance and Body Build Reveal a Lot

Apart from non-verbal cues, the appearance and body build also tells us a lot about the personality of the other person. Individuals having robust well-rounded figures with a tendency towards shortness and stoutness and whose chest and shoulders are rounded, neck and limbs are short and stocky, face is full, smooth, and shield-shaped are inclined to be genial, talkative, uninhibited individuals who enjoy social contacts. Their approach to problems is practical and realistic. They express their emotions freely and warmly, but at times they become unduly elated or depressed.

Individuals who have thin, flat, delicate physiques, are slender, have long lean limbs and flat narrow chest, head often elongated and facial features that are sharp, are inclined to be shy, reclusive, sensitive people who shun social contact and spend much of their time daydreaming. They are emotionally repressed and their approach to problems is theoretical and idealistic. Usually they are prudish and humourless.

Individuals, whose build is characterised by good muscular and skeletal development, including broad shoulders, large and long sturdy limbs generally have the same characteristics as mentioned for the thin, flat, delicate physique type.

Avoid Being Deceived – Recognising Deception

Now after having reviewed briefly the various non-verbal communication cues, the question of deception arises. Many a time, it becomes difficult to tell when others are being truthful or when they are lying. Here again we have to rely on non-verbal cues. Many such cues enable us to be at least moderately successful in recognising deception when it occurs.

First, we rely on ***micro-expressions*** – fleeting facial expressions lasting only a few tenths of a second. Such reactions appear on the face very quickly after an emotion-provoking event and are difficult to suppress. As a result, they can be quite revealing about the feelings and emotions others are actually experiencing.

Second, we rely on what have been termed as **inter-channel discrepancies**. These are inconsistencies between non-verbal cues from different basic channels; they result from the fact that persons who are lying find it difficult to control all aspects of their non-verbal behaviour simultaneously. For example, a negotiator who is lying to an opponent may succeed in maintaining an expression of open honesty on his face and may also succeed in preserving a high level of eye contact with the opponent. At the same time, however, he may engage in postural shifts or body movements or gestures like covering the mouth, that alert the opponent that something else is going on.

Third, we rely on changes in the non-verbal characteristics of people's speech. When people lie, the pitch of their voices often rises and they often speak more slowly and with less fluency. In addition, they engage in more sentence repairs – instances where they start a sentence, interrupt it, and then start again.

Finally, deception is often revealed in various aspects of eye contact. Liars blink more frequently and often show more dilated pupils than persons telling the truth. They may also show an unusually low level of eye contact or – paradoxically – an unusually high one, as they attempt to feign honesty by looking others right in the eye.

Through careful attention to these non-verbal cues, we can often tell when others are lying. Our performance in this respect is far from perfect – skilful liars do often succeed in deceiving us. But their task can be made difficult by our ability to read, interpret, and use a wide range of non-verbal cues.

Quick Summary – Beauty or Beast

In summary, person perception is the process through which we attempt to understand other persons. To obtain information about the temporary causes of behaviour, e.g. others' emotions or feelings, we focus on non-verbal cues. These are provided by others' facial expressions, eye contact, body postures or movements, and touching. Non-verbal behaviour plays an important role in social interaction. It is often used for purpose of self-presentation – to create a particular impression on others. In addition, through the use of non-verbal cues, we can often recognise when others are attempting to deceive us. □□

BODY LANGUAGE

One's current mood and emotions are often reflected in the position, posture, and movement of one's body. Together, such non-verbal behaviours are termed as **body language**, and they provide us with several useful kinds of information about others. Most of the basic communication gestures are the same all over the world. When people are happy, they smile; when they are sad or angry, they frown or scowl. Nodding the head is almost universally used to indicate 'yes' or affirmation. Shaking the head from side to side indicates 'no' or negation, and is also universal.

The evolutionary origin of some gestures can be traced to our primitive animal past. Baring the teeth is derived from the act of attacking and is still used by modern man in the form of a sneer and other such hostile gestures, even though he will not attack with his teeth. Smiling was originally a threat gesture, but today it is done in conjunction with non-threatening gestures to show pleasure.

The shoulder shrug is also a good example of a universal gesture that is used to show that a person does not know or understand what you are talking about. It is a multiple gesture that has three main parts: exposed palm, hunched shoulders and raised brow.

Just as verbal language differs from culture to culture, so does the non-verbal language. Where one gesture may be common in a particular culture and have a clear interpretation, it may be meaningless in another culture or even have a completely opposite meaning.

Each Gesture is an Unspoken Word

Like any other language, body language consists of words, sentences and punctuations. Each gesture is like a single word and a word may have several different meanings. It is only when one puts the word into a sentence with other words that one can fully understand its meaning. Gestures come in 'sentences' and invariably tell the truth about the person's feelings and attitudes. A 'perceptive' person is the one who can read the non-verbal sentences and actually match them against a person's verbal sentences.

Another important aspect in reading body language is that *all gestures should be considered in the context in which they occur.*

Non-verbal research has revealed a correlation between a person's command of the spoken word and the amount of gesticulation the person uses to communicate his or her message. This means that a person's status, power or prestige is also directly related to the number of gestures or body movements he uses. The person at the top end of the social or management scale can use his range of words to communicate his meaning, whereas the less educated or unskilled person will rely more on gestures than words to communicate.

The Palm Language

Throughout history, the open palm has been associated with truth, honesty, allegiance and submission. Generally, people use two basic palm positions. The palm facing upwards which shows submissiveness and the palm facing down, which shows dominance. An honest person will expose all or part of his palms to another person. On the other hand, a liar will hide or conceal his palms.

The palms are also used for shaking hands and a handshake can tell a lot. A dominant handshake is one in which the other person turns your palm in such a way that your palm is facing downwards in relation to the other person's palm. When both palms remain in the vertical position the feeling of mutual respect is transmitted.

Rubbing the palm together is also a mode of non-verbal communication. The speed at which a person rubs his palms together signals who he thinks will receive the positive results that are expected.

The Hand Language

When the hands are clenched together it indicates frustration. It signals that a person is holding back a negative attitude. The hands clenched gesture has three main positions: hands clenched in front of the face, hands resting on the desk and hands placed in front of the crotch when standing.

When the clenched hands are held high (at face level) it indicates the strong strength of his negative mood. Such a person will be more difficult to handle.

The Arm and Leg Language

During an emotional state, we all either respond positively with intense gestures or build up defences with subtle gestures depending on our evaluation of the situation and other related factors. Two of the gesture defences that we erect are the arm and leg barriers.

By folding one or both arms across the chest a barrier is formed that is, in essence, an attempt to block out the impending threat or undesirable circumstances. The arm barrier also reflects a person's nervous, negative or defensive attitude.

However, at times we also get to see people who partially cross their arms. A *partial arm-cross barrier* (when only one arm is used) reflects lack of self-confidence. We also at times have noted that people hold their own hands. This gives them emotional security. Psychologically, this gesture is a regression to that period in childhood where the person experienced emotional security when his parents held his hands under fearful circumstances.

Like arm barrier gestures, crossed legs are a signal that a negative or defensive attitude may exist. The purpose of crossing the arms on the chest was originally to defend the heart and upper body region, and crossing the legs is an attempt to shield the genital area. Crossed arms also indicate a more negative attitude than indicated by crossed legs, and the arms gesture is more obvious.

In the *standard leg-cross position* one leg is crossed neatly over the other, usually the right over the left. This gesture may indicate either a nervous, reserved or defensive attitude. One must interpret this gesture taking into account other gestures also and not in isolation.

When a person is sitting with crossed legs and crossed arms this means that he or she has withdrawn from conversation.

A leg-cross gesture can also at times indicate that an argumentative or competitive attitude exists. This is generally there when the legs are crossed in such a manner that they make the number 4. When a person locks this leg-cross gesture with one or both hands he is indicating tough-mindedness and stubbornness.

People often stand with their arms and legs crossed. This gesture is an indication of defence against personal space invasions and reflects their tensed state.

When a person has a defensive attitude, he not only locks his arms and legs but also his ankles at times. Males generally also clench their fists resting them on their knees or grip the arms of the chair tightly. Females, on the other hand, hold their knees together; their feet may be to one side and their hands rest side by side or one on top of the other, resting on the upper leg.

The foot lock is another important gesture reflecting a defensive attitude in women. In this gesture the top of one foot locks around the other leg to reinforce their defensive attitude. If you happen to come across this gesture, you will have to use a warm, friendly, low-key approach to bring the lady out of her shell.

The Courtship Gestures and Signals

Now we will discuss some gestures and signals, which are of interest to both the sexes. These are the courtship gestures and signals. Moreover, males tend to have fewer courtship gestures as compared to females.

A male-female encounter is an emotion-arising state and physiological changes are bound to occur. The muscles get toned up, 'bagging' around the face and eyes decreases, body sagging disappears, the chest protrudes, the stomach is automatically pulled in, potbellied slumping disappears, the body assumes an erect posture and the person appears to become more youthful in appearance. These changes are common in both the sexes.

The males, in addition to the automatic physiological reactions, exhibit some physical gestures and signals. Have you ever noticed a male in the company of a female/s. If not, do it next time and you will note that if he is wearing a tie, he will be reaching for his throat to straighten his tie. If the tie is not there then he may be trying to smooth his collar or brushing imaginary dust from his shoulder and rearranging his cufflinks, shirt, coat and other clothing. Other than these, he may even preen himself by smoothing his hair.

Clusters In Courtship Gestures

Courtship gestures generally appear in clusters. A sexually aggressive male will express himself by putting his thumb inside his belt thus highlighting his genital region. He may also turn his body towards the female and point his foot at her. At the same time, he will gaze at her intimately and try to hold her gaze for a split second longer than normal. If he is really keen, his pupils will be dilated. He will stand with his hands on hips to accentuate his physical size and show his readiness to be involved with the female. When seated or leaning against a wall, he may also spread his legs to give a crotch display.

Women are gifted with the art of courtship gestures and signals. They not only have the ability to send but also to read them more effectively as compared with the male. But alas! Very few males can pick up the signals being sent by interested or uninterested females and act upon them.

Most of the basic gestures used by women are the same as men – touching the hair, smoothing the clothing, one or both hands on hips, foot and body pointing towards the male, extended intimate gaze and increasing eye contact, a subtle thumbs-in-belt gesture, dilation of pupils and a flushed appearance in the cheeks.

The Tantalising Signals of the Female

Other than these common gestures and signals, the female arsenal is loaded with some real tantalising signals. Have you ever observed a female tossing her hair back over her shoulders or flicking it away from her face? If she is with you or around you, then you may be lucky. She is trying to catch your attention. Further, if she is really interested, you will notice that she will gradually begin to expose the smooth soft skin of her wrists – the wrist area is one of the highly erotic areas of the female body. Along with exposing the wrists she will also be making her palms visible.

The leg gestures of the females also give tantalising signals. When a female is interested in a male, she opens her leg wider in his presence than she would do under normal circumstances. On the other hand, a sexually defensive female will keep her legs crossed and together at all times.

Another typical female gesture is the rolling of the hips when walking. This gesture seems to have an innate origin as most of the females knowingly or unknowingly roll their hips while walking.

Subtle Courtship Gestures of Females

The slightly subtle courtship gestures of the females include – sideways glance, mouth slightly open, wet lips and application of lipstick to highlight sexual arousal. Along with this, they may be fondling a cylindrical object, or giving a sideways glance over their raised shoulders.

Other signals used by women include crossing and uncrossing the legs slowly in front of the man and gently stroking the thighs with her hand, indicating a desire to be touched. This is often accompanied by speaking in a low voice.

No Doubts – Actions Speak Louder

No doubt actions speak louder than words. Now I believe you are prepared and well armed to understand, court and get the one you love. So let's move ahead, start understanding the meaning of love, and then finally entering and conquering one personal zone after the other. □□

LOVES ME – LOVES ME NOT

Love is a complex emotion, a mixture of pity, sympathy, affection, and love and prominently sex. It has been suggested that a friendship between a man and a woman is transformed into love when the two individuals begin to perceive themselves as potential sexual partners. That is why love is believed to be the emotion aroused by sexual instinct. Love is also sometimes manifested as a permanent emotional tendency as in the case of a mother's love for her child. At this stage, it generally transforms into a sentiment. Selfishness and selflessness may be found in love in different degrees, as both are commonly present in it. Being a complex emotion, the external changes in love are extensive and they depend on the nature of the person, the intensity of love and the surrounding conditions.

Liking and Loving – The Difference

Another important aspect is the difference between liking and loving. There are at least three differences between liking and loving. First, fantasy seems to be an important component of *romantic love*. Many people enjoy fantasising about an ideal lover, but few spend any time fantasising about an ideal friend. *Obsessive thoughts and fantasies are the foremost characteristic of romantic love*. A second difference between loving and liking is that love is more likely to be associated with conflicting emotions – emotions of love and hate. A third difference involves the effects of time. Our liking for someone tends to increase as we spend more time with him or her, while romantic love appears to be a rather short-lived emotion. *An impressive number of experts argue that liking is a better basis for marriage than romantic love because the latter fades with time.*

The Romantic Ideal

A majority of people in our society subscribes to what is called the romantic ideal. That is, they believe they will fall in love with someone, marry that person, and live happily ever after in a state of romantic bliss. Of course, most people realise that often things do not work that way, but they nonetheless think that is the way things should work.

Who are more Romantic – Men or Women?

It is also generally believed that women are more romantic than men. Women are thought to be the ones who are seeking someone to fall in love with. Once married, they are the ones who try to maintain the romance in their relationship.

Men, on the other hand, are generally *thought* to be more interested in sexual than romantic gratification. Surprisingly, however, the research evidence suggests just the opposite; *men are more romantic than women*. Men are more likely to enter a relationship based on the desire to fall in love as compared with women. Also, men are found to be more distressed than women by the end of an affair and are more likely to suffer from feelings of guilt, depression, loneliness, and unhappiness. This is perhaps due to the fact that men refuse to believe that a relationship has ended and hold on to the hope that the woman will realise that she loved him after all.

Research (1999) done by Professor Helen Fisher at the Rutgers University and as reported in *The Times of India* dated 1st December, 1999, suggests that relationships between men and women are genetically programmed to self-destruct after four years. Majority of women are ready to leave their men shortly after the marriage service. Their genes tell them that children fathered by a series of men, creating a multiplicity of talents, stand a better chance of survival. The man may be playing around, but it is the woman who needs to move on to her next partner in a lifelong chain of serial monogamy. The brain chemicals that make us fall in love run out after 36 months, and it usually takes another year for one to realise this, look around and get out. However, don't get dejected because affection and warmth allows a relationship to thrive longer. All I have to say at this point are the lines I remember from a song *"Let it grow, let it grow. Let it blossom, let it grow"* and let not love be Tina Turner's second hand emotion.

How Love Happens

Now how does love happen? What all goes on in constituting the emotion of love? The emotion of love depends on the internal physiological arousal and external cues that suggest a label for the arousal. Thus, people will be especially susceptible to love when they experience a state of physiological arousal and find themselves in a situation that suggests that 'love' is an appropriate label for what they are experiencing.

Bodily arousal can be caused by either positive or negative experiences. Thus, fear, frustration, and rejection as well as positive experiences, such as sexual arousal, excitement, and joy, may influence the intensity of love. On the basis of this, we can say that love can lead to agony as well as ecstasy. Another interesting finding based on this is that love is usually the longest when the loved one is frustrating or rejecting his or her lover. This is so because humans have a tendency to strive for those desires which remain unfulfilled.

Defining Love

Now after this microscopic examination and evaluation of the emotion of love, we are in a position to try and define love. *Love can be defined as a state of intense absorption in another*. Sometimes 'lovers' are those who long for their partners and for complete fulfilment. Sometimes 'lovers' are those who are ecstatic at finally having attained their partner's love, and momentarily, complete fulfilment. It is also a state of intense physiological arousal.

Love Styles – How Do I Love Thee?

In many events, romantic love often begins as a sudden, intense, all-consuming response to another person. This kind of interpersonal response is labelled as passionate love, one of the several varieties of love that have been identified. A person experiencing passionate love tends to be preoccupied with his or her partner – and to perceive the love object as being perfect. Responses include sexual attraction, physiological arousal, the desire to be in constant contact, despair at the thought of the relationship ending, and the intense need to be loved in return.

Under the 'right' conditions, passionate love can arise suddenly and without warning, possibly accompanied by the secretion of neuro-chemicals that produce feelings of excitement and happiness. Even a brief contact with a stranger can sometimes lead to love at first sight.

Three conditions are required for passionate love to occur. First, you must learn what love is and develop the expectation that it will happen to you. The second condition required for the occurrence of passionate love is the presence of an appropriate target person with whom one can fall in love with. The third requirement is that states of emotional arousal occur while the love object is present.

Now if you live in a culture that teaches you what love is, meet someone who is an appropriate love object, and if you are physiologically aroused, you may very well interpret your arousal state as indicating love. But I am sorry to say it's not love. This type of love, which we have labelled as passionate love, is not very different from sexual desire. Sadly enough, this passionate love of yours is not likely to last long. Enduring love requires a more realistic foundation.

Despite (or because of) its intensity, passionate love is not long-lasting. Fortunately, there are other kinds of love that can be sustained over time.

Companionate love involves not the dazzling and dizzying emotional state of passionate love but the affection we feel for those with whom our lives are deeply entwined. This type of love represents a very close friendship in which two people are attracted, have much in common, care about each other's well-being, and express reciprocal liking and lead to a satisfactory long-term relationship more often than passionate love does; but companionate love does not lead to romantic songs and stories.

In addition to passionate and companionate love, there are four additional varieties or 'love styles'. Table II presents the elements of this six-part model of love with examples of test items designed to measure each type.

Research based on this model has found that men score higher than women in both passionate (Eros) and game-playing (Ludus) love. Females score higher than males on friendship love (Storge) and also on logical love (Pragma) and possessive love (Mania).

How Do I Love Thee? Six Possible Ways

This table indicates the six 'love styles' and presents sample items from a scale designed to measure each of them. People differ in the kind of love they feel, so the question of love style is a crucial issue for a couple attempting to work out a relationship that is satisfying to both.

TABLE II

Basic Love Styles	Sample Test Items
Eros: Passionate Love	My lover and I were attracted to each other immediately after we first met.
Storge: Friendship Love	Love is really a deep friendship, not a mysterious, mystical emotion.
Ludus: Game-playing Love	I sometimes had to keep two of my lovers from

contd...

	finding out about each other.
Mania: Possessive Love	I cannot relax if I suspect that my lover is with someone else.
Pragma: Logical Love	It is best to love someone within a similar background.
Agape: Selfless Love	I would rather suffer myself than let my lover suffer.

Game-playing love seems to be the least satisfactory type, in that it leads to relationship dissatisfaction and failure. Those who favour a game-playing approach to love tend to be concerned primarily with themselves and their own autonomy and self-fulfilment. However, it must be noted that romantic partners tend to be similar to one another in the kind of love they express.

Why People 'Fall' In Love – 'Rise UP'

There are Motivations

Have you ever wondered why people fall in love in the first place? Four kinds of motivation for falling in love have been identified – *distress* (loneliness, anxiety, low self-esteem), the need to *enhance self-identity* (wanting someone who could be helpful in developing one's artistic, intellectual, or professional skills), *ageing and social pressures* (the sense that others are romantically involved and one's social clock is ticking), and finally *sexual desire* (physiological arousal). *Each of these facilitators of love is associated with a specific love style*. Different facilitators probably lead to the selection of quite different kinds of partners.

The Three Basic Components of Love

Still another conceptualisation of love describes it as consisting of three basic components. The *first component* is **intimacy** – the closeness two people feel and the strength of the bond holding them together. Partners high in intimacy are concerned with each other's welfare and happiness, and they value, like, count, and understand one another. The *second component*, **passion**, is based on romance, physical attraction, and sexual intimacy. The *third component*, **decision/commitment**, represents cognitive factors such as the decision that one is in love and the commitment to maintain a loving relationship. *If, in a love relationship, passion is the primary component, the relationship tends to be short-lived; intimacy and commitment are essential to a lasting relationship*. Table III shows this ***triangular model of love***.

The Triangular Model of Love

According to this model, and as mentioned above, love is a triangle of three basic components: *intimacy, passion* and *decision/commitment*. Love can be based on any one of these alone, or combination of any two components, or on all three.

(A) There are seven quite different types of relationships, depending on which components are combined.

TABLE III

Liking = Intimacy Alone
(True friendship without passion or long-term commitment)

Romantic Love =
Intimacy + Passion
(Lovers physically and emotionally attracted to each other but without commitment, as in a summer romance)

Companionate Love =
Intimacy + Commitment
(Long-term committed friendship such as a marriage in which the passion has faded)

Consummate Love =
Intimacy + Passion + Commitment
(A complete love consisting of all three components – an ideal difficult to attain)

Infatuation = Passion Alone
(Passionate, obsessive love at first sight without intimacy or commitment)

Empty Love = Decision/ Commitment Alone
(Decision to love another without intimacy or passion)

Fatuous Love = **Passion + Commitment**
(Commitment based on passion but without time for intimacy to develop – shallow relationship such as a whirlwind courtship)

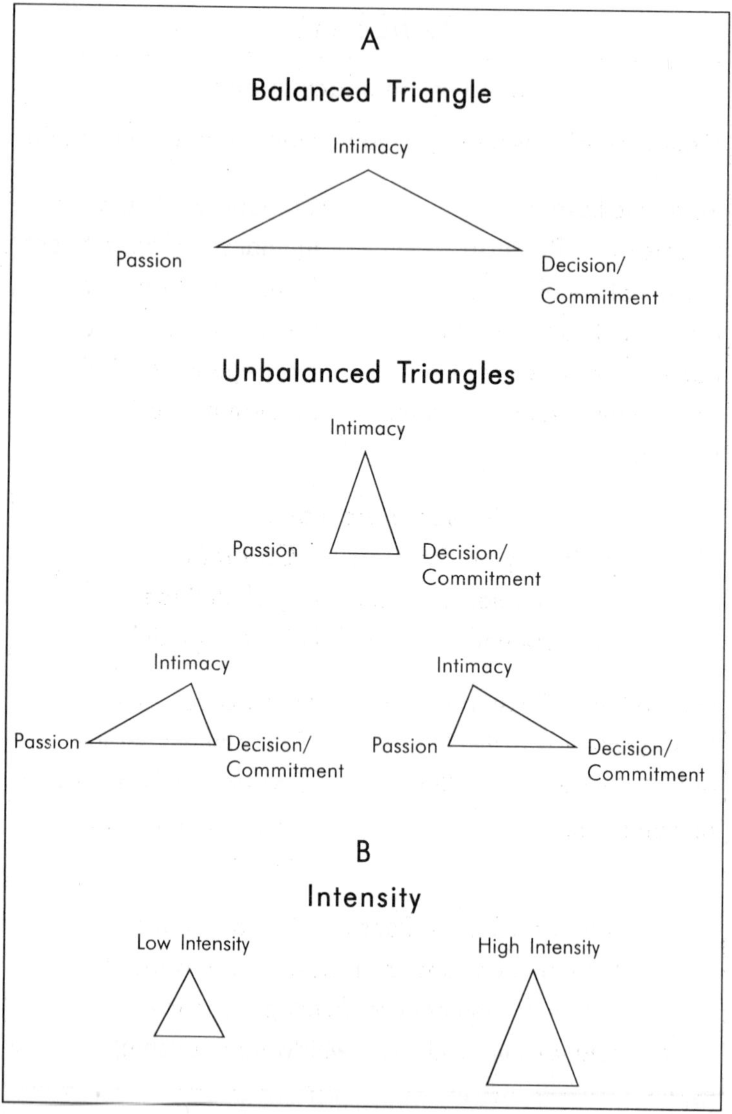
A
Balanced Triangle
Intimacy
Passion
Decision/
Commitment
Unbalanced Triangles
Intimacy
Passion
Decision/
Commitment
Intimacy
Passion
Decision/
Commitment
Intimacy
Passion
Decision/
Commitment
B
Intensity
Low Intensity
High Intensity

(B) The shapes of the triangle indicate the extent to which the three components are balanced.

(C) The size of the triangle represents the emotional intensity of love for an individual.

Love for Sex Vs Sex for Love

Another thing that needs to be talked about is on what basis people are attracted to a particular kind of romantic partner. Is the attraction primarily a sexual one, or is it based on the desire to form a close, loving relationship? In part, the answer is based on individual differences in a specific personality disposition. Socio-sexuality, a personality dimension, helps in measuring the type of attraction. At one extreme of this dimension are individuals of both sexes who have an unrestricted *socio-sexual orientation*, a willingness to engage in sexual interactions with partners even in the absence of closeness, commitment, or emotional bonding. At the other extreme are men and women who have a restricted *socio-sexual orientation*; for them,

RESTRICTED VERSUS UNRESTRICTED SOCIO-SEXUALITY

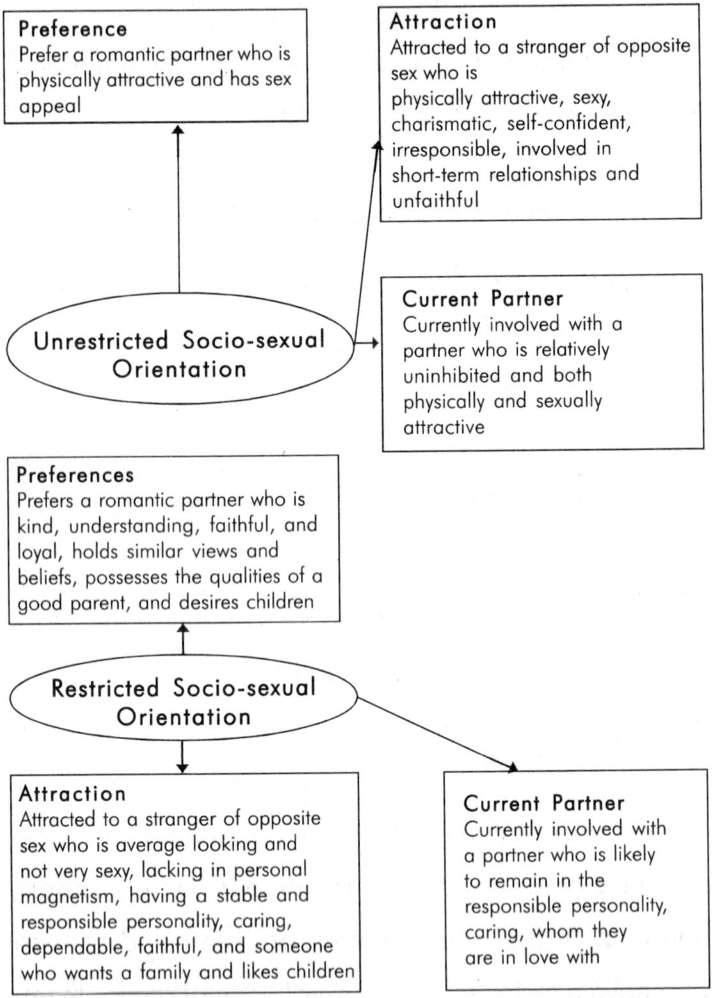

a sexual relationship must be based on feeling close, committed, and emotionally bonded. An unrestricted orientation is more characteristic of males than of females, but both extremes are found in both sexes.

Tests conducted indicate that compared to restricted individuals, unrestricted persons engage in sex earlier in a relationship, require less love and closeness, and are more likely to be involved with two or more partners simultaneously. These orientation differences are unrelated to sex drive, sexual satisfaction, or sex guilt and anxiety.

It is predicted that unrestricted individuals respond to fitness cues and prefer an attractive, sexy partner, while those with a restricted orientation would respond to commitment cues and prefer a partner on the basis of relevant personal characteristics.

It seems clear that restricted and unrestricted individuals would like to have, express a preference for, and actually become involved with romantic partners who differ in attributes involving commitment and parental investment (someone who is kind, affectionate, responsible, loyal, and faithful) versus reproductive fitness (someone who is physically attractive, sexy, and socially visible).

At some point in most relationships, passionate love begins to fade, and each individual must face the reality of spending his or her life with someone who is less than perfect. People who believe they are really ideally suited for one another can discover that there are negative as well as positive elements in the relationship.

Upsetting Behaviours in Love – Their Resultant

Some behaviours are generally upsetting to both sexes, while others are more annoying to one sex than to the other. Generally, women become upset if their partners are not loving and gently protective, while men become upset if their partners reject them sexually or ignore them. It should be noted that some people are more likely than others to behave in ways that cause a partner to be angry and upset. Individuals who are characteristically disagreeable, emotionally unstable, and/or unperceptive are more likely to evoke conflict. Also, those who characteristically fear being exploited in interpersonal relationships have greater difficulty in establishing and maintaining them.

When partners belatedly realise that they are dissimilar in some of their attitudes, values and preferences, negative feelings often arise. One of the problems with passionate love is that the overpowering emotional state in which *'love is blind'* makes it difficult or impossible to pay attention to such seemingly irrelevant details as the other person's similarities and dissimilarities to oneself. *One obvious solution for the two individuals is to know as much as possible about one another early in the relationship*.

Distress in Long-Term Relationships

For some, a long-term relationship becomes a source of distress because it is boring. Many dating couples report breaking up simply because they become bored with one another. When boredom arises, it can sometimes be overcome if the couple seeks new stimulation in the form of vacations, joint educational efforts, unfamiliar dining experiences, new hobbies they can share, new sexual practices, and so on. The alternative – continuing to do the same things in the same way – can easily lead to dissatisfaction.

Be Sure not to **Fall** but **Rise** in Love

To conclude this chapter, I would like to remark that make sure never to fall in love blindly. Try to let a relationship grow and slowly blossom. Develop a deep understanding for each other. Let not the foundation of love be laid on passions. Have a deeper, stronger and meaningful base. Then only the house of love you are building brick by brick will stand the test of time. Proceed to the next chapter and find the guidelines for building your house of love. □□

THE LINE OF CONTROL

Long time back while in school I had read a book on essays and what I still remember from one of the essays is a line – "Your *freedom ends where my nose begins*". Now years after I am re-thinking on this line, not in terms of prose but psychology.

The concept of personal space has existed since creation. Adam, Eve and all animals co-existed in harmony in the Garden of Eden till the forbidden fruit was tasted. Thereafter, territories were demarcated with clear, defined boundaries. The inhabitants of each territory shared an intangible allegiance to it and turned to savagery and killing in order to protect it.

Even today every individual has an area or space that he claims as his own, as if it were an extension of his body. Each has his own *personal territory,* which includes the area that exists around his possessions, such as his home which is bounded by fences, the inside of his motor vehicle, his own bedroom or personal chair. Rights to admission are strictly restricted and reserved around this air space.

Now to understand and evaluate behaviour in its totality, we must take into account the individual and his environment. An individual is in constant interaction with the environment around and within him. Many a co-existing fact determines the behaviour of an individual at a given moment.

The Concept of Life Space

First we will try to understand the interaction of the internal environment or psychological environment with the external environment and discuss about the concept of life space. *Life space refers to the psychological field and is employed to indicate the manifold co-existing facts which determine the behaviour of an individual at a given moment.*

Life space is a product of the interaction between the person and his environment. By person, three things can be implied – as equivalent to the 'life space' itself, in reference to the individual in the life space, the 'behaving self', and finally, as a direct reference to the psychological properties of the individual. In the last sense, a 'person' is extended to incorporate the needs, beliefs, values, and perceptual and motoric systems, which, during interaction among themselves and with the objective environment, produce the life space.

The word 'environment' refers both to the objective and the psychological environment. The psychological environment, or the environment as it exists for the individual, is a part of the life space. Its properties are determined by the characteristics of the person as well as by the characteristics of the objective environment. A region of the psychological environment may often be considered attractive or repulsive by the individual when this particular quality is absent in the objective environment.

Since the introduction of the concept of life space, the idea that it is pointless to speak of behaviour without reference to both the person and the environment has become commonly accepted. To understand behaviour requires not only knowledge of the person's past experiences, but also knowledge of present attitudes, capabilities and the immediate situation.

The Concept of Personal Space

Equally important is the concept of personal space in understanding behaviour. All of us tend to keep regular interpersonal distances when interacting with others. We stand closer or farther away from other people, depending on who they are and the nature of the interaction. Personal space may be thought of as a 'bubble' of space that we have around us and consider our own property. If another person violates our space, we may be uncomfortable or even angry.

Personal Space and Interpersonal Distance

A casual observation of people conversing can show some of the dynamics of personal space and interpersonal distance. If two acquaintances are talking and one of them leans too close to the other, the other is likely to compensate by backing up, thereby increasing the distance between them. By the same token, should the distance between them become too great, one will quickly narrow the gap by moving closer.

Edward Hall (1959), in his books *The Silent Language* and *The Hidden Dimension* (1966), coined the term **'proxemics'** to denote the study of people's use of space. Hall called our attention to the message we submit by the way we perceive and structure space. In his book *The Hidden Dimension,* Hall defined four interpersonal distances, or spatial zones, that people observe in their interaction with others. Each is divided into a near and a far phase.

The *first zone* called intimate **distance** or **zone** ranges from 0-18 inches. The near phase is the zone in which lovemaking or direct physical aggression takes place. The far phase is used for interactions in which touching is permissible and in which conversation is carried on in very low voices.

The *second zone*, **personal distance** or **zone** is 18-48 inches, a distance that comfortably separates two individuals. It is the distance of social interaction between friends that do not involve physical contacts. The near phase of personal distance, for instance, may be the distance people maintain at a crowded cocktail party.

The *third zone*, **social distance** or **zone**, extending from 4-12 feet, is used in more formal interactions where personal involvement is substantially reduced. It is the distance people use to insulate themselves from others. Business persons maintain this distance in their interactions. Hall observed, for instance, that desks in office of company presidents are large enough to keep subordinates or visitors at the far phase of social distance. This distance may also be used for interviewing applicants or conducting formal negotiations.

The *final zone* is **public distance** or **zone**, the near phase of which extends from 12-25 feet away from the person. Communication at this phase is always quite formal and is essentially one-way. Hall believed that interpersonal distances beyond 25 feet preclude any possibility of interaction. A distance of 25 feet or more is almost automatically set around important public figures when they deliver formal presentations.

Personal Space – An Indicator of Relationships

One of the most important determinants of the use of personal space is the relationship that exists between the individuals. In general, the more intimate the relationship, the closer people stand. Friends stand closer than strangers and men and women who are sexually attracted to each other stand closer than friends. Having an infinite amount of personal space can at times be very stressful.

Personal Space as Indicators of Personality Factors

Personality factors also affect our use of space. People with certain personality disturbances tend to use larger interpersonal distances. Normal persons with high achievement motivation keep larger personal spaces than less achievement-oriented persons. Another personality correlate of spatial behaviour is self-esteem. Individuals with a positive self-concept approach others more closely than those with a negative self-concept do.

Personal Space and Gender

Studies on sex differences suggest that men require more personal space than women; you almost find them standing closer than men. However, sex differences in interpersonal distance must be considered in terms of whether persons of the same or opposite sex are interacting. A number of studies have reported that male-female pairs are usually closer to each other than same sex pairs. The sexes also differ in their reactions to violations of personal space. Males generally appear to be more upset than females when their personal space is invaded, although both sexes are bothered.

Personal Space and Cultural Differences

Cross-cultural differences also exist in the use of personal space. Germans are known for their large zones of personal space and are supposedly less flexible in their spatial behaviour than Americans. Germans go to great lengths to protect their personal space with heavy walls, solid fences, and closed doors. Mediterranean Europeans and Arabs, on the other hand, display a great tolerance for closeness and prefer to maintain 'intimate' or 'personal', distances.

Similarities among members of a given group tend to produce closer interpersonal distances. Also, individuals of the same race tend to interact at closer distances than individuals of different races. It has also been observed that lower-class individuals maintain closer interaction distances than those from the middle class.

Personal Space Intrusion – Its Consequences

Conflicting preferences in personal distances can have important consequences, especially when people interact on a regular basis. Our intimate zone is normally entered by another person for one of two reasons. First, the intruder is a close relative or friend, or he or she may be making sexual advances. Second, the intruder is hostile and may be about to attack. While we will tolerate strangers moving within our personal and social zones, the intrusion of a stranger into our intimate zone causes physiological changes to take place within our bodies. The heart pumps faster, adrenaline pours into the bloodstream and blood is pumped to the brain and the muscles as physical preparations for a possible fight or flight situation are made. This is a typical physiological reaction. If you want people to feel comfortable in your company and behave naturally without emotions attached, the golden rule is 'don't infiltrate the line of control' because your freedom ends where their nose begins – the size of nose does vary from individual to individual. The more intimate our relationship is with other people, the closer we are permitted to move within their zones.

Using the Concept of Personal Space – Get the One You Want

Now how do you use the concept of personal space in understanding one's behaviour and getting the one you want? For this purpose, vital information is needed, and this can be had by territorial invasion techniques that break down the resistance of the individual in question. Encroaching into the intimate and close intimate zones when asking questions and carrying on till they are answered can do this. It often takes only a short while for this territorial harassment to break down the individual's resistance. But alas! It's not everyone's cup of tea. Many technical aspects are involved in this breaking down process. This we will deal with in detail in the last chapter. Before we come to that, another important thing is breaking the ice, which we will discuss in the next chapter. □□

BREAKING THE ICE

(Theoretical Model of Intrusion)

In this chapter, I present before you a theoretical model of intrusion developed by me, based on psychological concepts and a lot of personal experience and research done by me. The knowledge that you acquire after going through this theoretical model will prepare you for the final intrusion in practical terms.

Build the Bridge of Confidence

The first and the most essential step I feel is building the bridge of confidence. This is essential as every individual has erected defences around him and is put on alert at the slightest hint of intrusion. Now how does one build this bridge? There is no theoretical model as such or blueprint available so far. In my opinion, the entire operation has to be carried out smoothly by modes of communication – verbal as well as non-verbal. If we don't know the individual, first we have to invade into his/her public zone. Communication at this zone is always quite formal and one-way. Now the question of the skills that you should possess arises.

Skills Required by You – Equip Yourself

Your skill largely lies in your basic knowledge about human beings. You must keep *three things* in mind: First, individuals differ in their ability to respond, second, individuals differ in their readiness to respond, and finally, individuals differ in their motivation to respond.

Thus, the same technique will not do for all people because of individual differences. We need to know the basis on which individuals differ as far as the persuasive techniques of intrusion are concerned.

1. Identify and Fulfil the Needs of the Target Person

Human beings are like other organisms. They have *needs* – some weak, some strong – that must be at least partially fulfilled at various times for satisfaction in life. The problem is to identify these needs systematically because it is an essential aspect of intrusion. Humans have various kinds of needs which emerge and re-emerge as they are fulfilled.

At the bottom of the hierarchy are the most urgent physiological needs, including hunger and thirst. Unless these needs are satisfied, we are unlikely to worry about higher level needs such as safety, belongingness, self-esteem, or self-actualisation. Other than these, a number of meta-needs exist. These are truth, justice, order, meaningfulness, beauty, and unity. In contrast to the basic needs, meta-needs co-exist rather than being arranged hierarchically.

You have to capitalise on the whole notion of human need levels, that is, you should know what needs or drives the one you want needs fulfilment of. Relying on this, you have to base your communication process of moving into his/her heart, aiming your communication at satisfying that need. Suppose you feel that the one you have given your heart to lacks love, belonging and affection, then your communication must be so that it aims to satisfy these needs. Your success will depend in large degree upon your ability to assess the need of the one you want with accuracy and thereby impressing upon him/her that you are the one who can satisfy those needs.

2. Avoid being Incongruous

Another important aspect is *consistency*. All human beings want a resolution of psychological and interpersonal conflict and have difficulty tolerating incongruous elements in their worlds. You have to avoid creating any type of conflicting situations and show resolution with their thinking. Suppose your future partner is against the concept of a love marriage and you express your love or desire to marry her in the very initial stage of the relationship, chances are that she may get scared and step back. Take your time, and it's best to go with her thinking till you feel you have addicted her with your love – then break the ice.

3. Make the Heart Rule over the Head – Genuineness will Help

This process till now may look like a cakewalk, but beware, humans are bestowed with the capacity to think rationally, to act purposefully and to deal effectively with their environment. You must keep in mind that the person you are trying to woo is also an intelligent human and can very well make out your moves. You have to be genuine in all that you do to impress the other. This genuineness will help you in overcoming the resistance which intelligence puts up. The crux of this is that make the heart rule over the head.

4. Use Pure Emotional Reactions – They are Genuine

One of the best approaches would be to arouse the other person emotionally, and sweep the one you admire and love off their feet. These days, the best way of arousing emotional feelings is through the short message services of the mobile phone. Send emotionally charged messages and generate within the other the feelings you want to be generated. Being original will make your messages sound more genuine. However, a word of caution: If the receiver does not respond to your initial messages, stop sending them or else they may negatively affect your relationship.

5. Use Your Natural Charms to Impress

Your personality is an important and decisive factor as far as breaking the ice is concerned. You can use your positive personality traits to influence upon the attitudes, beliefs, values, etc., of the one you are wooing. Different people have different personality traits, which naturally emerge when one is trying to woo someone. Sometimes even a smile can make a lot of difference and at others, your manner of conversation can help create the wanting impression. So search within yourself and bring out the best of your natural positive charms.

The Qualities You Must Possess – Your Arsenal

We will now discuss the personality qualities and skills that you must possess. Any normal communication situation for you will include three basic elements, namely *source* (which is you), *channel* or *message*, and *receiver* (the one you want to be yours). *In order for you to be persuasive in nature, your communication situation must involve a conscious attempt by you to intrude into the personal space of the one you want through the transmission of verbal or non-verbal signals. The chief concern here is the characteristic of effective communication mode that you must process or the personality quality of yours.*

Your arsenal should have a combination of three components – *credibility, attractiveness* and *power*. The impression, which will be formed upon the one you want, will enhance the process of intrusion via any of these three aspects. These three will lead to the breaking of defences of your attractive and stimulating target – this is a well proven and researched fact of persuasive psychology applied in various areas of persuasion.

Your Credibility is Important

Who you are and what you are is going to make a major difference in identifying your credibility. No one will interact with complete strangers till they are assured of his/her credibility. You need to be someone or someone needs to know you and introduce you to the one you wish to propose to in due course of time. Your credibility will also be reflected in your expertise, your intelligence, your objectivity, your apparent motives through all that you do and say. For example, you may get fascinated with a person travelling with you in a train but you cannot even dream of having a long-term relationship with him/her without establishing your credibility or evaluating that of the other. So the first thing you need to do is establish your credibility.

You Need Different Types of Strategies – Plan Them

The expertise with which you direct and redirect your communication aimed at persuading the one to give his/her heart out to you is also an extremely important aspect. The fast changing horizon of society, which includes various fields, requires different types of persuasive intrusion strategies, and under such circumstances, you need to be an expert persuader who is intelligent enough and skilful in the art of persuading people via communication using various strategies. As part of expertise, you should also be equipped with the sense of knowing when to use and when to withdraw a particular strategy.

You Need to be Objective in Your Views

Another dimension of your credibility is its objectivity. You must be objective in your views; otherwise, you may not be able to invade effectively.

Work on Your Language Style

The style of your language as well as the way of delivery also has a persuasive importance. A dynamic, pushy style will produce more suspiciousness of your good and pure intentions. In contrast, a subdued style will produce magical effect in most of the cases.

Some Success will be Motivating – It Increases Efficiency

It has been well researched that when the needs of humans get satisfied to some extent, they are self-motivated to achieve beyond. If you begin to achieve success in your love mission in the initial phases, then you will surely be able to penetrate beyond the social zone, and be highly motivated to function more effectively.

Familiarity and Similarity may Lead to Liking

Your attractiveness, as a component and factor of persuasion, has three aspects – *familiarity*, *similarity* and *liking*.

There is considerable body of evidence that a person is influenced by a persuasive message to the extent that he perceives it as coming from a source similar to himself. Thus, if there is similarity between you and the one you intend to woo, it will work like a magnet and increase the attractiveness ratio between the two.

It has also been proved that liking would be an inverted U-shaped function of familiarity. There will be maximum liking when familiarity is of intermediate degree.

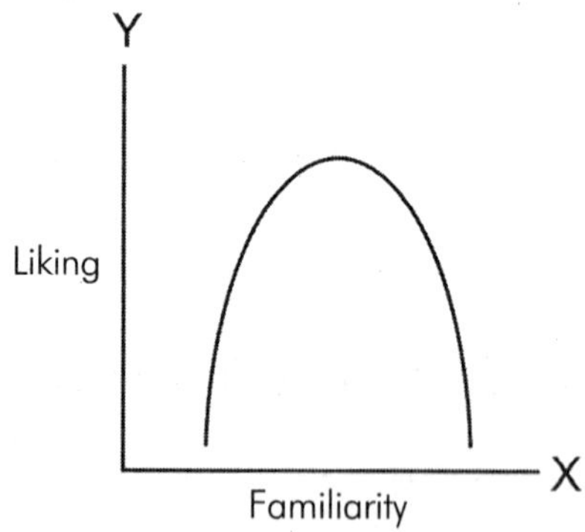

It would seem unobjectionable to hypothesise that the more the one you intend to woo likes you, the more he/she would change his/her belief towards the position you are advocating and not resist intrusion into his/her personal space.

It is however interesting that some psychological studies predict just the opposite relationship: that under certain specified conditions, you can produce more opinion change as the dislike of the one you intend to woo increases towards you, i.e. your future love will hate to love you but surely love you!!!

The Power to Sanction – Rewards and Punishments

Another important factor involved in helping you break the ice is your power to sanction (means and end control over reward and punishment) and will strongly help you in the persuasive intrusion into the personal space of the one you intend to woo with all your love. Your power can be considered to be effective in intrusion if you keep concern about the other person's compliance. Try giving more of rewards and less of punishments, because by rewarding you will win and by punishing, lose.

Some General Aspects

From the above analysis, you are now well acquainted with the various characteristics you should possess for effective intrusion. Besides these, some other aspects must also be taken into consideration, for instance age, sex, etc.

It is a general belief that as age increases, the experience also does. But this is not always true. In many a situation, a young person can be proved much more effective as compared to an older or middle aged person provided the younger one is much skilful in that specific field. At times, persuasive intrusion requires experience over energy and enthusiasm from the intruder. So, generally speaking, under these circumstances an aged person would be more effective than a younger one. You must have noticed that young boys and girls go in for the older lot. Experience does count. But don't lose heart and wait for age to catch on. Exceptions are always there!!!

In more specific situations, sex can be considered as a dimension of intruder effectiveness. Females can generally intrude into other female's personal space since females as such require less personal space as compared to men. For men to intrude into the personal space of women depends on the various aspects discussed. These aspects are need, emotion, intelligence, personality, credibility, attractiveness, power, expertise, etc.

WIth this we can sum up our discussion, keeping in mind that your personality traits are an effective element in the persuasive intrusion process in one's personal space, and that it consists of multifarious dimensions and a proper combination or interaction of all the stated factors in order to make intrusion effective. □□

THE FINAL INTRUSION

PUBLIC ZONE TO SOCIAL ZONE

The general strategy behind personal space intrusion is though quite simple but the process complicated. Before one can start intruding into the other's personal zone, it is essential to **identify the emotional needs of the other person**. Emotional needs include the need for attention, the need for understanding, the need for acceptance, the need for appreciation and the needs for love, belonging and affection. The identification of emotional needs helps, since people subconsciously grow dependent upon those who satisfy their emotional needs. One needs to cash on this basic fact and try to fulfil the required need/s.

Fulfil the Need for Attention

The first need is that of attention. Who in this world does not desire to catch attention of others? Hence one must show the other person that you are consciously aware of his or her existence. A smile, a compliment or just an admiring look may spark off the beginning of a relationship, but not necessary a long-term one, since this is just a superficial need and once satisfied, the other more important needs take over. But do remember, never let the person concerned feel your lack of attention else he/she will seek it from elsewhere and your chapter may end here itself.

Understand the Feelings and Emotions of the One You Want

As said before, just making a person aware of his or her existence is not enough. One also needs to show that they understand the other person's feelings and emotions. The ability to understand and to some extent share the experience of another person's feelings depends greatly upon the ability to interpret an individual's expressive behaviour. This in turn seems to depend upon a genuine interest and concern for that person. So here is a warning to those who do not have patience. Don't try to hurry up things else the reaction may become opposite. Be a smooth operator and take your time understanding the other person and then only express yourself in accordance.

Always Express Worthiness

Acceptance is another important emotional need. People desire to be liked and loved and to belong. It means showing the person that you value being with him/her, even though at times their behaviour or attitudes may be less than praiseworthy.

Always be Appreciative – It's an Incentive

A life without appreciation would virtually be a life without incentive. Whatever we do, we consciously or unconsciously seek appreciation. You can satisfy this need by recognising those redeeming qualities that the other person possesses. But again there is a note of warning. Appreciate the realities or else it turns into flattery, and many people get turned off by it.

Always Show Your Affection

Even the most ferocious of horses can be tamed by showing affection, and human beings are no exceptions. What people desire most is affection. This is easily shown by reassuring the person that, regardless of comparisons with others, he or she is still special to you and, therefore, very important. Sometimes this can be communicated by no more than a simple touch.

As you begin to meet a person's five basic emotional needs, you start helping that person along the road to greater happiness. In return, he or she will develop a subconscious emotional dependence on you. This dependence is an essential part of personal space intrusion. In order to encourage persons to voluntarily place this trust in you, however, you must first prove yourself worthy of their trust.

Always Show Respect

Apart from trying to meet the basic emotional needs of the other person, it is also important to respect that person. This is so because people are motivated to be with and to associate themselves with those persons whom they truly respect. This respect can only be had on a mutual basis. A basic fact that must be kept in mind is that respect is always commanded and never demanded. One respects those who are perceived as independent and self-reliant. The more a person seems to be capable of getting along in life without having to rely on us, the more likely we are to actually feel drawn towards that person.

Maintain a Distance – Don t Stick Like Glue

Another point of importance to be kept in mind is that people are most attracted to those who exhibit some degree of aloofness, are self-reliant and independent. Thus one must never show to the other person that he/ she is indispensable for you.

Show Continued Interest

Showing continued interest in the other person is also important. This can be conveyed by a smile, by looking lovingly deep into the other person's eyes, by greeting them vocally, by starting and being able to maintain a meaningful conversation, and finally fixing up the next meeting. Don't give up even if you feel the pace is slow. You will surely succeed and capture the victor's cup, but patience is the key to success.

Having successfully accomplished our mission so far, we are now ready to proceed further into the personal zone. However, an important tip remains to be given at this stage. When one is striving to form favourable impressions, then the best way to succeed is by letting the others know that you are favourably impressed by them.

SOCIAL ZONE TO PERSONAL ZONE

Though people have a subconscious need to stay free and emotionally uncommitted, they will try their level best to avoid circumstances which threaten to limit this freedom. This basic concept should be kept in mind when one prepares for the intrusion from social zone to personal zone. It is important that one has to hold himself and strike only when the iron is hot. Let the other person mentally prepare himself/herself for readily allowing you to intrude into their personal zone.

Let your Actions Speak Louder than your Words

The best way to succeed in the above strategy is by letting your actions speak louder than your words. With passage of time, you will succeed in breaking the barriers and develop a more intimate relationship. But don't undermine the importance of words. Pick and choose the spicy yet loving words and whisper the same as and when appropriate. This is entirely your cup of tea. How you manipulate your verbal gestures depends on your understanding and evaluation of the situation in its totality. Hence, you are the judge as well as the judged.

As the experience becomes more positive and beneficial, the greater becomes the desire of the other person to continue with the association.

Some Basic Rules to Make You Rule

One cannot be forced to like someone since, under normal conditions, the human mind cannot be forced into doing things. But if one cannot force, one can at least lead it to do the desired task at will. There are some basic rules that are to be followed to achieve this objective, and the magic will coax any person you choose into enjoying and looking forward to the pleasure of your company.

Always be Cheerful – Keep Smiling

The first basic rule is to always be cheerful. Cheerfulness is very infectious. It lightens the environment and the people around, and tends to be emotionally stimulating and rewarding.

Along with cheerfulness is closely associated the smile. This is the second rule. A smile sure goes a long way and is a must at every stage of intrusion. A smile is the most effective key to being attractive, especially to members of the opposite sex. With a smile even the toughest of tough melt. It's the greatest weapon in your artillery, but not scarce, so use it freely and abundantly.

Be Enthusiastic

The third basic rule, coupled with the two mentioned before, is enthusiasm. It's a natural outcome of genuineness and is very infectious too. It breeds excitement in others. It is a very helpful and positive mode by which people can be influenced. So be enthusiastic and pump enthusiasm into others. This act of yours will reflect your genuine care and concern for the one you are reaching out to.

Control Your Verbal Communication

The fourth rule applies to verbal communication. This, as mentioned earlier, is a very crucial aspect. A six-inch tongue can kill a man of six feet. So don't just say what comes to your mouth. Think and then only speak and make sure it's positive, loaded with subtle humour. Out of personal experience, I have found that the best way of verbal communication in situations like this is to use a subtle, subdued and romantic tone. You should make the other person feel that you are speaking your heart out. But one warning comes with this. Don't overdo the act or else repulsion may occur for anything excessive is never good. So change your track from time to time. Try to discuss the other person's interests giving him/her more opportunity to express himself. Don't try to be dominating always. This way you will be able to gather more information about that person.

Under-stay Your Welcome

Another golden rule is under-staying your welcome. Though this is not an easy task but very essential. If one stays for too long, he starts losing the charismatic appeal that has been built up so far. Over-exposure is never good. So leave them high and dry. Leave them wanting more of you. People will enjoy your company more, as a result of having you available less. Also try to do a vanishing act. Don't turn up at times when you are expected. This adds fuel to the fire of passion, especially when dealing with the fairer sex. The gist of this is plain and simple. People respect and are subconsciously drawn towards those who exhibit qualities of aloofness and independence. They are repulsed by those who manifest tendencies to cling.

After having successfully manoeuvred the personal space intrusion so far, you are now ready for the final assault of moving from the personal zone into the intimate of intimate zones and for which you have to induce emotional dependence. So let's march ahead and conquer and captivate

the heart, mind and soul of the one we so desire – at least theoretically!

PERSONAL ZONE TO INTIMATE ZONE

Moving from the personal zone to the intimate zone is dependent on and influenced by many factors. These factors range from caste, creed, race, to society, family, peers, religious philosophy, etc. All these influence the mental set-up and attitude of an individual. It can lead an individual to be conservative or liberal. However, in most cases, the rule is that your freedom ends where the nose of the other begins – the sizes of the nose do vary. Anyway there is no harm in working out a theoretical model of intrusion into the intimate zone. I would however like to warn – *don't try to use it for vested interests and for gratifying your evil needs. Respect the feelings of others and proceed only if you are genuinely interested in them.*

It's a fact that people become emotionally dependent on those who can truly satisfy their never-ending need for human understanding. Thus, ***the key*** *to intrusion is getting the other person emotionally dependent on you and not vice-versa.* Now how do you go about doing this? The tactics discussed ahead will help you accomplish this mission.

Make Yourself Available

The first and foremost requirement is that of availability. Make yourself available to the one you want. Make your presence known and felt. This is essential since people tend to fall in love with those who are relatively closer at hand. However, as warned earlier, don't stick around like glue. Be around when you feel the other person needs you – a need which you have already induced.

Learn to Listen

The second requirement is that of *reflective listening*. This can be one of the most successful ways to strengthen your relationship with others. A few tips related with this are being given below.

1. The first golden rule is observing silence while the other person is speaking.
2. Restrict your body movements since movements lead to division of attention. You surely want it to be captured.
3. Give feedback through head nods as they reflect acknowledgement on your part. Restrict your comments to "yes, go on".
4. Your eyes should be focussed on the speaker all the time. Direct eye contact would be the best.
5. If the speaker pauses for some response from your end, try briefly summing the contents in an accurate manner.
6. Avoid passing negative remarks or judgements on what the person is saying. You can do so at a later stage.
7. Don't pressurise the person to finish speaking soon. Give space for their expression.

Thus, the more understanding you provide for the one you want, the greater influence you will have with that person. In addition, that person will become more strongly attached to you. The importance of reflective listening as a tool in your arsenal to win the other cannot be emphasised much upon. It is perhaps the most essential tactic of all to include in your overall strategy of personal space intrusion.

Satisfy the Need for Acceptance

Another important aspect concerns the strength and intensity of feelings. Studies and experience tell that the intensity of feelings one person will experience towards another in a relationship occurs in direct proportion to how important and worthwhile they believe they are in the eyes of that other person. The more important a person feels than he or she really is to you, the stronger and deeper will be their reciprocated feelings of love, dependence, and attachment for you. This is the need for acceptance, which every human needs satisfaction of.

Admiration Works Wonders – Keep Complimenting

Another important need, which needs fulfilment at this stage of intrusion, is the need for admiration. A mirror can only produce an image. It cannot express beyond. It is here that you take over. Let your eyes be the mirror, which not only reflects but also expresses. Look deep and lovingly into the eyes of the other person and express your appreciation. Try to appreciate the uncommon aspects and use the most unthinkable of compliments. You do need rehearsals prior to this but be very spontaneous when you enact the same. If you make a conscious effort to satisfy this need then they will develop a deeper dependence on you. They will no longer ask the mirror who the fairest and most beautiful of all is. It's naturally going to be you and not they themselves.

Supply Sympathy Whenever Required

Supplying sympathy is also an essential part in intrusion. Many a time, people try to project that they do not need sympathy but this is just a reaction formation. In reality, people do need sympathy. So make it a point to extend a loving hand and whisper a few words of encouragement when you feel it is required. This will help to relieve their emotional burdens and strengthen the bonds of attachment that they feel for you. A process of osmosis takes place by virtue of which you will find the other gravitating towards you. However, heed this warning. Don't make the other person feel as an object of pity. It may harm his self-esteem and in turn harm your relationship. The best way to offer sympathy is by sharing the emotional, imbalanced state of that individual. Make them feel that you feel for them and are sharing their feelings with the same intensity.

Spend Time on Retrospection

Now we are slowly but steadily inching towards our goal. When you reach this stage, a few important questions are to be asked and answered by you. Are you getting the fulfilment you desire from the relationship? Is the other person responding in the way you want? Do you want to carry on with the relationship beyond this point? If your answers are 'yes', then proceed further. If they are 'no', then it's time to put on your thinking cap. There are other fish in the sea waiting for you.

The next steps are for those who are sure they want to carry on beyond and it's time also for the final assessment of the other person's feelings for you.

Bring in Some Insecurity – It leads to Vulnerability

It's a psychologically acclaimed fact that the more insecure a person feels about where he or she stands with you, the more vulnerable he will be to your advances, and the more intensely he will desire you. So let's go about theoretically (practically in your case) examining this hypothesis.

People can never fully appreciate someone's love and concern if they are allowed to take that love for granted. There must be some ongoing apprehension that the love and concern so freely given could be lost at any time. People become absolutely frantic with desire when they feel the danger of losing what they possess. This concept is now to be put into use to successfully stir up the emotions of the other for you as well as to gauge the passion they have for you. So lead them to believe that they could lose you forever and create a feeling of insecurity in them. Insecurity is the mother of infatuation and is symbolic to adding fuel to fire – the fire of passion.

How to Create Insecurity

How do you go about creating this feeling of insecurity? The first thing is that you must feel secure for yourself, i.e. you must have confidence that you will not lose the one into whose intimate zone you are preparing to intrude. So first prepare yourself and then proceed.

The *first* golden rule is silence. So far you have been verbally expressing yourself and trying to meet the various needs of the individual by setting up a two-way communication network. Now one line has snapped and the network is working one-way. How bugging it can be when your telephone at times works this way. The same holds true in a relationship. Silence creates an emotional imbalance and starts generating a sense of insecurity. Imaginations start running wild giving jitters. There is nothing more powerful than wild imaginations for creating the feeling of insecurity we want to create. So sit back, relax and enjoy the situation. But don't cut the communication totally. Try to make small talk and keep the person guessing.

Nothing – absolutely nothing – else can turn a person's disinterested, uncaring attitude around and make them burn with feverish desire for your company because of the fear of being dumped. Try to exhibit a brush off attitude. Signal non-verbally your feelings of detachment from them and see how they crawl on their knees (if they really love you). The fire of passion is catching a flame but it still needs some more fuel. Now before going further it's time for assessment and judgement. Observe the reactions of the target person. Are they conducive to your intrusion process? If not, it is time to mellow down a bit, and if yes then it's time for adding more fuel.

Create Rivalry – It will Stir up More Desire

Nothing can create more feelings of possessiveness than jealousy. So create some competition. Socialise with friends of the opposite sex. Flirt with them. A little rivalry can stir up a person's hot-blooded passion and desire for you.

Give Some Reinforcements – They are Love Saving

At this stage, it is also essential that we give some reinforcements. We have to keep the person's romantic passions alight. One must thus give a few sparks of hope showing that you still reciprocate their feelings. Failing this you might end up as the loser instead. Romantic infatuation is a delicately balanced human response. It thrives on uncertainty. On the one hand, too much self-confidence in a person will kill excitement. On the other hand, no confidence at all will starve it to death. So while keeping the one you want from any certainty that you are hooked on them, you must still provide them with some glimmers of hope that you might become so. So resume contact after a temporary lull in the relationship. Ring them up. Visit them but for a very short period. After a few days go out with them. Now make your interest shift from cold to hot. Enjoy the stronger bonds you have been able to tie successfully.

Thus, by backing off from a relationship that you have been aggressively pursuing for some time, the other person will automatically let down his or her emotional guard and, thus, become more vulnerable to your renewed advances.

Strike when the Iron is Hot

Now it is the right time to intrude into the intimate zone. The iron is hot and it's time to strike. Awaken the much desired physical attraction, since the exhilarating experience of 'falling in love' is unquestionably a sex-linked phenomenon. Whether you are consciously aware of it or not, the mainspring of all romantic activities is the instinctive sexual drive of the human species. Its constancy and strength is what keeps husbands and wives and consequently families, together in the first place. Without it, few people would be sufficiently motivated to commit their entire lives to another individual in such an exclusive arrangement as that of marriage.

Now how do you go ahead with this exciting task? You will have to take the initiative if your partner does not do so. You will have to be the aggressive one. Your success will lie on the firm foundations of love and respect, which you have already established.

A Simple Touch can do Magic

Every one desires the warmth of physical affection and human touch. Make sure the one you want is comfortable with your physical closeness by engaging in non-sexual touching first. Sometimes, however, the person you have designs on may be uncomfortable either expressing or receiving physical affection. If so, then gradually 'condition' a person to being touched by you. But be very patient. Begin by touching the person in a non-sexual way – hold their hands – briefly, from time to time whenever you are engaged in conversation. In time, gradually increase the duration of contact, as well as the frequency. A person's back, shoulders, and arms are generally safe, non-threatening parts of the body that can be touched with little risk of a traumatic emotional response.

Start the Appetisers

Eventually, however, you must move on to the real thing. Here start with the appetisers – the kiss. Kissing stirs up passions. Kiss the hands first and then proceed to the cheeks, forehead, eyes, nose, chin and finally the lips. Closely observe the reaction of the other. Compliment the other with each kiss you give. Make sure there is initially no passion in your kiss. Your job is to stir up the passion in the other first. To make this job easy, try the feet (of the fairer sex). Most people are not aware of the stimulating power of the feet in a woman. It is symbolic as well. Each lady wants to be treated like a queen – a queen of your heart. Try to overcome any resistance by smooth talking. Show that you don't desire the other person sexually. You are not being sexually stimulated by them. Relax and see how it works.

If You Fail – Don't Use Force

However, if it does not work relax. Don't get worked up and try to force yourself onto the other. Carry on with normal conversation as if nothing has happened. Later, in the quiet hours of reflective contemplation, the seeds of desire will begin to grow. The one you want will begin to fantasise about what it might have been like if..., and the next time they will.

Love is an Understanding, It's Not Sex: Beware and Become Aware

My final words to you would be 'Beware and become aware' of the consequences of indulging in pre-marital sexual relationships.I have to warn you as a responsible citizen of a country that has a rich cultural heritage and also as an arbitrator of moral and social conduct. As a psychologist, I come across many counselling cases, which confirm the wisdom of the counsel I give to you. In the present Western set-up, it is very easy to arouse emotions and instigate flames of passions but without you being aware they burn out too soon and only the ashes remain of the relationship based purely on sex. Sex and sensuality are like credit cards, if in the wrong hands and misused cause enough of pain and trouble. Pre-marital sex destroys chances of developing any real sense of commitment in the relationship. Many innocent, gullible girls get used by men who profess profound love for their lust. Many couples mutually agree for the pleasures but they ultimately infect and destroy the building process of any long-term relationship.

All young and old want to indulge in sex today. We mostly have sex on our mind all the time. The force behind it drives us and it is dominating and directing our lives to a great extent. Though the sexual satisfaction mechanism of the female is much complicated and complex but very seldom this force drives only a few of them. Men long for more and in variety, and indulge in it to boost the male ego. But does it really give men a sense of worth within, a feeling of happiness and worthiness? This reflects on the primitive animal instincts which man has carried forward with him through generations. It reflects on the insatiable pleasure wants, which obey the pleasure principle without taking reality into consideration. It reflects on one's inner being – a soul in search of happiness through bodily pleasure. This dominant drive has far reaching implications for both personal and social living. It can make us do degrading things out of which we seek pleasure. It can destroy us if we do not monitor and control it properly. AIDS is a glaring example and the outcome of this drive without reins.

I would like to conclude with a prayer meant for each and every individual "God grant me the serenity to accept the things I cannot change, courage to change the things I can, and wisdom to know the difference." □□

WISH YOU ALL THE BEST

Do write to me for advice and guidance at samvaidhna@hotmail.com. As a psychologist, I would love to hear about your experiences and counsel you if so required by you: ***Take my advice, I don't use it!!!***